T5-AGW-117

The Practitioner Inquiry Series

Marilyn Cochran-Smith and Susan L. Lytle, *SERIES EDITORS*

ADVISORY BOARD: JoBeth Allen, Judy Buchanan, Robert Fecho,
Susan Florio-Ruane, Sarah Freedman, Karen Gallas, Andrew Gitlin,
Dixie Goswami, Peter Grimmett, Gloria Ladson-Billings,
Sarah Michaels, Susan Noffke, Marsha Pincus, Marty Rutherford,
Lynne Strieb, Carol Tateishi, Diane Waff, Ken Zeichner

(continued)

"What About Rose?"
Using Teacher Research to Reverse School Failure

Smokey Wilson
Foreword by Glynda Hull

Teachers College, Columbia University
New York and London

Published by Teachers College Press, 1234 Amsterdam Avenue,
New York, NY 10027

Copyright © 2007 by Teachers College, Columbia University

All rights reserved. No part of this publication may be reproduced or transmitted in any
form or by any means, electronic or mechanical, including photocopy, or any information
storage and retrieval system, without permission from the publisher.

Library of Congress Cataloging-in-Publication Data

Wilson, Smokey, 1941–
    What about Rose? : Using teacher research to reverse school failure /
Smokey Wilson.
        p. cm. — (The practitioner inquiry series)
    Includes bibliographical references and index.
    ISBN 978-0-8077-4787-2 (pbk. : alk. paper)
    ISBN 978-0-8077-4788-9 (cloth : alk. paper)
    1. Remedial teaching—United States. 2. English language—Remedial
teaching. 3. People with social disabilities—Education (Higher)—United
States. 4. Effective teaching—United States. I. Title.
LB1029.R4W55 2007
371.9′043–dc22   2006103034

978-0-8077-4787-2 (pbk : alk. paper)
978-0-8077-4788-9 (cloth : alk. paper)

Printed on acid-free paper
Manufactured in the United States of America

14 13 12 11 10 09 08 07   8 7 6 5 4 3 2 1

To my children,
John, James, and Martena;
and to my grandchildren,
Cassidy, Troy David, Cole, Will, and Elijah.

Contents

Foreword

For the last 25 years the educational movement called "teacher research" has stretched and spread its wings. Conducting inquiries into their own classrooms, schools, and communities, teachers across the United States and around the world have claimed the right to and experienced the joy of investigating their practice. For their part, academicians, long considered the frosty guardians of knowledge generation, have begun to bless the emergence of teacher research and the consequent shiftings of roles and balances of power in researcher-practitioner relationships. Books have been written about methods and procedures for teacher research; articles have appeared in scholarly journals to describe its dimensions and locate its theoretical lineage; and edited collections of teacher research have been assembled that provide examples of its multiple forms and value. All of this is not to say that teacher research is a universally accepted paradigm; to be sure, it is contested or unsupported or simply ignored in various quarters, particularly given current institutional investments in accountability, testing, and standards, where little room seems left for agency, especially on the part of teachers. Still, in some important senses, teacher research has arrived; and with this new maturity, we might expect powerful and substantive and innovative examples of what it has achieved and thereby what it can promise. So it is with Smokey Wilson's *"What About Rose?"*

This book is many splendid things:

- a compelling illustration of a lifetime of research by a community college composition and reading teacher, conducted with her own students in her own classrooms
- an engaging autobiography of a teacher's worries, triumphs, and intense involvement with teaching and inquiry across a career, frankly and humorously revealed
- an incisive summary and critique, from a teacher's-eye view, of a half-century's most significant and controversial and sometimes wrong-headed theorizing about teaching and learning
- a gentle but direct guide for those teachers who would also be intrepid investigators of their own practice

- a collection of vivid, even unforgettable portraits of those adult students who found their way to her community college classes over the years

The hallmark of Smokey Wilson's research, and of teacher research in general, is its genesis in conundrums of practice. For her, the middle-class daughter of a liberal arts education in literature, the issue was how it had come to pass that her young adult and adult students, most of them African American and all from poor urban neighborhoods, had arrived at college ill-prepared for academic literacy demands. And, of course, she wanted to know what could be done to promote these learners' literacy growth. How might their school failures be transformed into successes, both in community college and in earlier schooling? Thus Wilson as a beginning teacher began to chart her decades-long exploration of some of the most troubling, recalcitrant, and important educational and social issues of our time. *"What About Rose?"* chronicles her journey.

The educational literature, and indeed our system of education in the United States, has not typically paid a great deal of attention to struggling adult students. To reach adulthood and not be able to read and write with some alacrity has long been a stigma in this country, solidly incontrovertible evidence to many that a person is simply not academically turned. In fact, federally supported educational interventions now focus on younger and younger children. It is well known that the educational consequences will likely be dire for a child who can't read by 5th grade; thus funding for special programs and services is front-loaded to the early years. But "What about Rose?" we hear Smokey Wilson ask, "Capable as an adult, and no doubt as a child, but silent and ashamed when she walked into a classroom?" What about those adult students who decide to make a fresh start, to invent a second chance, and who appear in community college classrooms, doubtful of their abilities and timid from memories of having been poor students, but driven nonetheless to succeed in school at last? Enacting the best traditions of teacher research, Wilson calls attention to issues and people and points of view that only those on the front lines of educational practice are likely to experience, value, and understand.

In this regard her work echoes the spirit and substance of two earlier books that have themselves become classics. Mina Shaughnessy's *Errors and Expectations* gave a whole generation of college writing teachers a road map for understanding and indeed appreciating the attempts by "underprepared" students—those suddenly admitted to college during the open admissions era—to write academic essays. In *Lives on the Boundary*, Mike Rose wrote a "hopeful book about those who fail," training the attention of academics, teachers, and the wider public, too, on the misread abilities and aspirations of students relegated to the remedial and vocational tracks. Mina Shaughnessy, Mike Rose, and Smokey Wilson share, then, a generative ability to find in students' prior histories of schooling the keys to the logic of their current unconventional literacy performances; they are each remarkably able, to borrow Mike Rose's phrasing again, "to shift the lens in order to see from others' points of view." These are habits of mind that certainly serve teachers and researchers still, and in *"What About Rose?"* they are enacted chapter by chapter.

Wilson's puzzlement over her students, both those who flourished in community college despite failing in earlier schooling and those for whom community college did not become a second chance, first sent her to the archives of educational research in hopes of finding helpful theories and approaches about turning students' academic lives around. In *"What About Rose?"* she relives her encounters with that literature and thereby re-creates the history of her experiences with now famous and infamous texts. Reminiscent of Michael Cole's approach in *A Once and Future Discipline,* that is, his reconstruction of the history of cultural psychology and his simultaneous account of his own role in the birth of that discipline, Wilson reviews chronologically many of the major players in educational thought, but always by asking, "What about Rose?" Juxtaposing the explanations that she found in the academic literature with her experience of students in her classroom, she realized that a sobering number of these influential theories were *themselves* lacking, particularly the early accounts of genetic and cultural deficiencies that had their heyday decades ago but still resurface on a regular basis, if in somewhat different garb.

Later Wilson encountered educational literatures more compatible with her predilections and more useful in theorizing her interactions with her students, and these guided her own set of studies in her classroom over several decades. Thus sections of *"What About Rose?"* read like a Baedeker of the last half century's social sciences: Bateson, Bowles and Gintis, Goffman, Gumperz, Labov, Lakoff, Ogbu, Searle, Vygotsky. Just as helpful as her summaries of their major contributions are Wilson's evaluations of the theories from the point of view of a teacher on the front lines. What comes across in these sections that is remarkable, and what points to the value of teachers being engaged in inquiry about their classrooms and students, is a mind actively, voraciously at work, seeking explanations and solutions. We have evidence here of what proponents of teacher research have claimed all along, and that is the ways in which inquiry can sustain engagement with teaching. Wilson's example, however, is most rare: an illustration of engagement both sustained and documented over an entire career. As one set of theories leads to another and as one classroom study suggests the next, Wilson re-creates the unfolding of her life as a teacher-researcher. In Mary Catherine Bateson's terms, one of the pleasures of reading this book is learning how an individual teacher "composed" a professional life, negotiating twists, turns, anguished dead ends, and hopeful paths born of sustained inquiry and a commitment to her students, and then using her example to reflect on our own professional directions, choices, and happenstance.

Teachers of writing have been especially active in the teacher research movement, and for them, *"What About Rose?"* will have unusual import. Smokey Wilson in fact began her research because she was puzzled at the difficulty students had in getting words on the page, and often she was equally and simultaneously struck by their dexterity in speech and performance. Taking a cue from the many research studies at the time that privileged the analysis of talk and honored the complexity of (mis)communication, Wilson read widely in social science literatures on resistance and reproduction and the ways in which schooling appears set up to continue the status quo. She rejected those accounts that simplistically reduced students' failures to inept and conspiring teachers yet offered no solutions or hope, and she located her own projects in the all-important writing conference, where she and her students met, interacted, and constructed the students' texts jointly. These moments, she was able to show through her studies, had great and grave significance for the eventual academic essays that students could create. With audio and video recordings used to capture word and gesture, some of the most poignant and memorable moments from *"What About Rose?"* are the transcripts that Wilson provides of writing conferences gone awry. In these moments we stand with her at the abyss that separated Wilson interactionally from her African American urban students. Differences in race, culture, social class, and gender shout at us from the page, yet we gradually come to see, as the sessions progress and the chapters unfold, the particular strategies that Wilson discovered whereby teachers can help students transform talk into written compositions.

Probably the greatest debate, the sorest topic, and the hardest problem of our lifetime to solve has centered on structure, agency, and social change, and the role of education within that process. *"What About Rose?"* is part of that conversation, a link in the chain of Bakhtin's theory of speech communication, the collection of turns that stretches across many disciplines and fields. It is easy at this historical moment to be discouraged, almost to abandon hope, given the state of many schools in the United States, not to mention the state of our larger world that is mired in conflict. Indeed, it does seem now that "things fall apart" and "the centre cannot hold," as Yeats lamented almost a century ago. The beauty of Smokey Wilson is that, unlike many insightful but ultimately chair-bound theorists who have written about social change over the past few decades, she points us to an avenue for action. I imagine it broad and tree-filled and welcoming. Like teacher-researchers before her, and, I especially hope, like the newly-inspired teacher-researchers who will come after, she brings to her understanding of structural constraints a hopeful vision, one based on the individual transformations she has fostered and witnessed in her classroom and that she now represents for us all in *"What About Rose?"*

—Glynda A. Hull
University of California at Berkeley

Acknowledgments

This book could never have been written without the students who brought to me their questions, their perseverance, and their achievements, and without the tutors who brought their insights to the many meetings we held. Of the many tutors, I thank most especially Awele, David, Teta, Rinda, Stephanie, and Patricia, all of whom participated in the talk-writing study. In order to protect the privacy of students and tutors, pseudonyms replace given names with the exceptions of the student in Chapter 5 and the tutors in Chapters 8 and 9, who all asked that their given names be used.

I am grateful to colleagues and friends Margot Dashiell, Susan Schacher, Ellen Hart, Dorothy Wilson, and Lucy Day; they helped Bruce Jacobs, Marlene Griffith, and me develop the original curriculum and pedagogy that became the Project Bridge model for adult basic reading, writing, and math students. Margot Dashiell and Susan Schacher, in particular, did much to reshape the program for issues of the new century.

I want to thank Susan Lytle, one of the editors for the Practitioner Inquiry Series of Teachers College Press, for asking me to submit a manuscript for the series; although it took a while, I never forgot the invitation. I also want to thank all those at Teachers College Press who turned a manuscript into a book.

Judith Faust, librarian at California State University of the East Bay (Hayward), found many of the sources that I had not had in hand for a decade or more. Most important, the manuscript would not have found its way to Teachers College Press in respectable form without the painstaking work, far beyond duty's call, of Jean O'Meara.

Just as those nearest to me have helped my work, I also owe appreciation to those whose ideas have been my inspiration. Some—like John Austin, Paul Grice, and Shirley Brice Heath—I have come close to through their teaching or writing. Others—like John Gumperz, Robin Lakoff, and Herb Simons—supported me in their roles as professors and advisors. A few have been both intellectual mentors and companions: Glynda Hull, Andrea Lunsford, Mike Rose, and Geneva Smitherman

shared my passionate interest in and concern for students like those described in this volume and offered guidance and encouragement over
the years.

All that said, without the almost daily support and collaboration of
Marlene Griffith, this book would have remained always a virtual reality.
And finally, I gratefully thank my mother, who at 93 remains my staunch
supporter, and my children for their patience and support throughout.

Introduction

STRANGER: So what do you do?
ME: I teach in a community college.
STRANGER: What do you teach?
ME: Reading and writing, you know, basics.
STRANGER: Why are you teaching *that* in college?

At get-togethers, when I answer the well-worn conversation opener with comments about teaching "students who had failed in high school," my new acquaintance often takes over the conversation, launching a discussion on the ills of American education, the loss of standards, the national disgrace. I have learned to stop with my first short answer. To open the topic for talk of social justice, critical literacy, and social stratification often turns casual conversation into hard-fought arguments. This book is the long answer to the question of "Why are you teaching *that* in college?"

I MEET UP WITH BASIC SKILLS

I have had a long time to think about my kind of work and what it means. From the time I was 16 I knew I wanted a career. By my first year in college, I knew it would be using text, either reading or writing. By the time I had my MA, I knew it would be teaching. But where that would take me, how I came to understand the magical act of watching texts change lives, was completely unexpected—Frost's path "less traveled by," after all.

After I finished my degree in Arizona and almost on the spur of the moment, my husband and I decided to go to California, for I had heard there were jobs there. The first contract I was offered was in an urban community college whose buildings had been World War II barracks. It was a long way from the green lawns and brick buildings where I had said farewell to my favorite professors in Arizona the month before. As I looked in the "brand-new" library, housed in a portable building, I would not admit to anyone, not even to myself, that I was in culture shock.

When 25 of us inhabited the tiny space with squeaky floors called the Reading Lab, it was full—very, very full—and noisy. I knew little—very, very little—about teaching people how to read. I got through the semester by watching through the glass in the door the teacher who had a reading class before mine. He was rumored to be a reading specialist, so what he did, I did.

Within a few months I discovered two things that turned out to be more important lessons than I realized at the time. First, I did not at all like the remedial reading supplies the college provided, which consisted of boxes of utterly bland reading/skill-drill cards that had been color-coded to indicate reading level. Second, I was charmed by the students who suffered through those skill cards with me. There must have been 15 skill levels, with 10 cards per level, and I found that work as daunting and dreary as they did. By November we began "just talking."

It was 1965, and the students were in school with the help of President Johnson's War on Poverty. At that time, few teachers at the community college where I worked were prepared for what "open admission" called for. Yet the students did not seem to hold that against me, and I had a special feeling about the place and the students. Along with the shabbiness of everything, there was a determination—a scruffy determination—to build something new.

Most of the voices I hear now from those early semesters are thankfully too mixed to be clear. The courses must have finished, and I must have learned something about teaching, since nobody fired me for incompetence. But what I do remember clearly were the times when the coach's prize basketball player, who usually stumbled over every word, suddenly read smoothly for a line or two and captured the "inner TV show" that I had said the words produced. Or the times when I saw the thunderstruck expression when students grasped the possibilities in what they had put on paper after having wrestled the writing to make the words say what they intended. The best moments were the times when, after working together on a tangled sentence, a student and I would both look up, surprised at just how good, how right, the sentence had become.

I was still largely shooting from the hip. If something I tried worked—or didn't work—I had no idea why. It took a long time to figure out that a love for language and a respect for language learners were necessary but not sufficient for doing a good job. I never regretted my graduate work in literature or my thesis on *King Lear*—both actually became useful—but I realized that this was only partial preparation for what I needed in order to work with students who had a history of failing in school and to convert that history into student success.

And so, after 10 years of teaching, I returned to graduate school to understand the two sides of the American education coin—success and failure. I needed to know why the remedial classes were almost always filled with African American students. Why were they almost never in the classes that were reading Thoreau's *Walden?*

The Students I Came to Know

They had been "school failers" in public education, but they were back in school, this time as adults ready for success. I knew this because students often began the semester by saying to me, before or after class, in low whispers, "I don't read so good," or "My writing's terrible." They hoped this time to repair the past by fixing the future. Our futures, then, and our search for success, became a single route.

I knew how I had arrived at that reading lab, but I knew little about my students. Who were they, who are they, these strangers to academic corridors? Some are now, as they were then, in their early 20s, others are nearer 40 or 50. All of them enter unsure of reading and writing long after the ages of 6 to 14, those years designated as the points of typical emergent literacy. They often fill the ranks of the working poor, have minimum-wage jobs, and see no way out except through education. Many have internalized a fear that they have some kind of inability to learn.

These students have neither mastered the rituals and processes of academia nor acquired the various levels, or layers, of literacy needed for college or for a career. As much as anything else they need to learn ways "to do" school, ways to adapt what they know to the literacies of college. To get an education, they must take and pass "basic writing" and "preparation for reading" in order to qualify for college-level courses like freshman composition and critical thinking and all those other milestones on the road to completing a degree or a certificate. And even before beginning, they must be savvy enough to decipher college schedules, to work with counselors, and to understand how to read between the lines of a placement test.

In general my students were serious and plenty smart enough to handle school, but they were vulnerable to criticism and often appeared either extremely shy or armored with the mask of "cool." As I started to see patterns, the questions multiplied and the answers divided. Some students reached December on the road to success. Others disappeared before Halloween.

Understanding School Failure: Seeking Answers

I had at least a dozen questions. Why did some learners succeed while others continued old patterns? What was the route from basic skills to academic literacy? For those who again became school-leavers, what interrupted the education they had returned to claim? For those who persisted, did school success in fact bring about life changes? And underneath it all, why hadn't the transformation that schooling is supposed to provide happened long before adulthood?

I hoped to find answers to my questions in graduate school. After all, a forest's worth of pages had already been written to try to get a grip on remediation. I envisioned a rich, reciprocal, and well-developed knowledge link, one coming directly from the university to our community college, and our learning with nontraditional students pouring new knowledge back into the university. I assumed this link between a world-famous university and a hometown community college, separated by not more than 20 miles, would already be in place. I was wrong.

In fact, in 1965 most university research in learning to read and write pertained to children, and much of it was housed in the discipline of educational psychology. The research did not mention the learners I had in mind and had not plotted what powered their trajectory into (or out of) education beyond high school. What was available in adult education was primarily curriculum and materials; no one was speculating on why adults needed elementary school instruction in a country of universal education, even though there were so many urban Americans who had fallen out of the system. There simply were no ready-made answers to my questions.

A way to approach my questions came to me as I listened to Robin Lakoff—a linguist/sociolinguist I much admired—lecture about women's language in Marin County. Now Marin is as different from inner-city Oakland as it could possibly be, but suddenly I saw how a researcher's insights into one sort of dialect could apply to other kinds of language variation as well. I realized that only by making the answers myself could I learn what had happened to the learners I knew best and discover how to help them. My questions were my own. My task was to create my own connections between theory and practice and then to find other classroom teachers and university researchers who were equally engaged in making this population more visible and more successful in schools.

Why Classroom Research Matters

This book will be useful for readers of various interests. It has much to say about teaching reading and writing to adults, those we have too often and too wrongly assumed are beyond the stage of language learning or academic development. It digests the theories and studies put forward over the years to explain the difficulties African American children (and their parents) sometimes face in our educational system, and presents in panoramic array the explanations of school failure spanning 50 years. Those who read detective novels for the thrill of the chase may understand that this is a mystery tale: a search for elusive answers that turn out to be complex and ambiguous (and remain so even now). But, most especially, this is a book for teachers who wish to study their own classrooms. For these readers the appendix, "Guide to Classroom Research for Teachers," offers support for their research processes, while the chapters describing my own research provide exemplars of the stages along the journey.

THEORIES THAT MATTER

Vygotsky's Influence

Teachers teach from theory, whether they recognize it or not, and the theory that has sustained and guided me throughout comes from the work of Lev Vygotsky. Born in Belorussia (now Belarus) in 1896, this psychologist, literary critic, and professor of medicine took special interest in inner speech and written language. He had much to say that related to my work: that writing, for example, is an internalization of social relations and an externalization of inner speech; that its developmental trajectory is both continuous and discontinuous, "recursive but not circular." By *developmental*, Vygotsky meant a "contradictory process," in that today's successes turn into tomorrow's failures—the problem to be solved at the next level of development (Zebroski, 1994, pp. 157, 161, 164).

The notion I borrowed from Vygotsky is the idea that learning occurs in the *zone of proximal development*. I visualize this space, this zone of so-near-yet-so-far. I see the teacher with certain kinds of knowing on one side of the zone, the learner on the other, and as-yet-untraveled land between. In order to meet, the teacher must make the first move, from the side of knowing. From the student's perspective, whatever the learning task, the trek looks global, impossible, endless. Yet the word *proximal* means "near." The teacher knows that the meeting place will turn out to be not so far away and the trek not so endless once the student engages with the task.

Various things can happen in the approach to the task across this landscape. The teacher may say what learners cannot hear, and learners may not be able to make explicit their questions. The teacher may lose patience, and the learner may decide to walk away. Or the approach can be smooth—if a teacher or a tutor sees the problems from the learner's view, answers questions just right, and shows the other where the road starts, both of them can gain a new foothold in development and in writing, or learning, or in teaching itself.

In my own work, I tried to connect with students and with students and text over and again. When I failed, certain actions, often communicative issues, created the difficulty. When I succeeded, I saw the migration of text from one mind to another.

Social Networks

A corollary to Vygotsky's zone of proximal development is the importance of social networks. The ability to read and write has long been equated with intelligence—wrongly equated, in my judgment. One may ask, "If you're so smart, why can't you read?" Or one may ask, "Since you're smart, why did the process start only now?" One answer to that question, I became convinced, is the intimate relation between literacy and social networks.

There are many variables, of course, that affect learning and communication in school. But one variable is more often than not painfully present: ongoing miscommunication between teacher and student correlates with classroom disengagement. If not repaired, the wall between learner and teacher grows steadily thicker and higher. Teachers need to be aware of where communication breaks down if they want to reach students behind the wall. Vygotsky pointed out that reading turns out to be related to who listens to us, and writing turns out to be related to who hears us.

What still stands, to the extent that anything still stands, is the significance of who talks to whom and which students receive special attention. Specifically, I have examined exchanges between teachers (or more accomplished peers) and learners. These teacher-learner exchanges convey how learning can happen effectively within school culture or how it can fail to happen. Such teacher-learner partnerships were rare in the childhoods of the students I bring to these pages. Then, even more than at present, many teachers had little space or time to develop and maintain such partnerships or to analyze the partnerships that failed.

What have I learned from all these semesters of studying my classes? I have learned how literacy is transmitted. I have seen again and again how print literacies migrate from teachers in painstakingly gained increments and come to belong to the students. Literacy is contagious, and students catch it interactively; they catch it from their teachers.

A Map Through the Volume

The book presents classroom studies I undertook between 1975 and 1995. One of its goals is to reveal not only what I found but how I found it. I have traced the processes by which this research unfolds in order to show the path from the first faint call of a question to that place where answers are found. Like the phases or stages of this research, the volume is divided into five parts: Getting Started, Finding a Focus, Collecting Artifacts, Analyzing Artifacts, and Writing It Up. With the exception of the last, each part contains two chapters.

Chapters generally include three sections: In Practice, In Theory, and In Response. In Practice presents a snapshot of classroom life that raised a particular question for me. Next, the In Theory section discusses the theories and experimental studies that helped me cast light on the problem. The third section, In Response, analyzes the various theoretical positions and weighs in on the advantages and setbacks each offered. A fourth section, In Retrospect, looks back at the moments in education history that the chapter outlines and considers how the global educational theories fit with the local, day-to-day teaching and learning for teachers like me and students like Rose.

A teacher's response to research must be, I believe, a check on theoretical notions and speculations in light of what our students show us to be right. Reading the theories behind the research in our field shows us how our thinking has changed as it moved from the hands of educational psychologists to psycholinguists, to sociolinguists, and to the anthropologists, ethnographers of communication, and conversational analysts. Given a panoramic view, we see how the complexity of the issue of school performance has built up layer by layer over the last 30 years in America's search for equity in schools. For the researcher, especially the teacher-researcher, it explores the range and depth of thinking that can help us "see" classrooms better. Answers change with better theory. Theory changes with better answers. Teachers need to be part of the changes for the better.

To promote that goal, I've included as an appendix the "Guide to Classroom Research for Teachers" as an aid for teachers who wish to do research within their own or their colleagues' classrooms. Someone new to research needs to know that there is a process that unfolds, and may need direction on how to begin, how to focus a question, what options there are when it's time to collect data, how to analyze the data, and what to do with the findings when the work is done.

As we reflect on our practice from the vantage point of classroom research, we understand clearly that no matter how we cringe from a mistake we made in teaching that day, as teacher-researchers we can also witness that mistake and use it as the growing end of learning.

On the basis of years of my triangular travel between problematic practice, library, and new inquiry, I can with confidence assure classroom researchers that they can trust the research process. No matter how often I stand against the unknown, if I just keep at it, the students help me unveil what was obscure and allow it to make sense.

Part I

GETTING STARTED

The two chapters in Part I—"Rose: Reversing School Failure" and "Mark: Repeating School Failure"—describe two students who came to college with similar problems but took different paths through basic skills classes that semester.

Similar students, different outcomes: What made these differences? When a teacher is left without a ready answer or when a teacher sees a dozen equally possible answers, then she is at the beginning of her research.

As the "Guide to Classroom Research for Teachers" (the appendix, hereafter called the "Guide") emphasizes, "Getting Started" is that moment when neither the answers nor the question are yet clear. Trying to decide what to examine and what question to ask is a difficult time in the research process; it may last a week or it may last half a year. But teachers often speak of "the epiphany" or the "moment I knew what I wanted to ask." The best advice probably is to remain open to the point at which key issues converge.

Chapter 1

Rose:
Reversing School Failure

How does someone like Rose—competent, mature, and ready to learn—arrive at a community college unable to read and write at a 10th-grade level?

IN PRACTICE

I still remember the students from the 1970s—ghosts now but still present in my research—Rose in particular. Her hair was not straightened and was dyed reddish-gold, her face was pixielike, her eyes were shiny, and her skin was caramel-creamy and blemish-free. I had gotten to know her well. I knew her neighborhood and the schools she had attended. I often watched her trudging along the cement passageways on campus, sometimes with children in tow, loaded with both books and child care supplies. Perhaps because my own children were the same ages, or maybe just because I thought she had many possibilities and too few opportunities, I had taken a special interest in her.

In class, Rose exuded confidence. She helped newcomers to the college find the bookstore and get settled. She exemplified the question that made me crazy: Why did so many of my students succeed in college when they had struggled dismally in their earlier years? I wanted to know what had gone wrong. Rose expressed an interest in writing about her previous English classes, and I hoped she would discuss her other school experiences as well.

In the early 1970s, talk about students' "voice" was everywhere. A committee of the National Council of Teachers of English, headed by Melvin Butler, prepared its famous member-approved resolution entitled "Students' Right to Their Own Language" (1974). According to Richard Larsen in the open letter that introduced the policy statement, the purpose of this special publication was to help teachers confront a major problem: "How to respond to the variety in their students' dialects."

I had long been interested in the voices of African American speakers—even when I had to use bulky reel-to-reel recorders to capture them. "Students' Right . . ." merely underscored what I already believed: A summary of Rose's story in my words would not be the same as that story in Rose's voice. I did not know then that relations between talk and writing would become important to me; I only knew I had to capture the nuances of what Rose said. Scarcely thinking about it, I set up a tape recorder. Rose seemed ready to begin writing, but she just sat looking at the blank page for a while. Just when I was about to prompt her with questions, she began to get her thoughts into words—and she began by talking rather than writing.

Rose spoke about her experiences politely but forcefully. I did, from time to time, ask a question, but often she ignored my prompts. She traced her problems to 10th grade, explaining that her schoolbook was "too hard for her reading level." Her memory was clear, even years after the incident took place. (In the dialog that follows, *Smokey* is the teacher's voice and *Rose* is the voice of the student. When speaking, Rose did not pause between her sentences. I have left out many periods in her speech to reflect the rushed nature of her speech.)

SMOKEY: You were gonna tell about that English class?

ROSE: Yeah and this teacher said everyone was gonna read out loud that day, and so every time it was my turn I'd kinda get in back of somebody, you know, because I didn't want to [read], and then when it was finally my turn, everyone else they stumbled, you know, but not as much as I did and I felt so embarrassed.

SMOKEY: Do you remember what . . . the book was you were reading?

ROSE: I was in 10th grade. I don't know why I don't remember, but it was a 10th grade book, and then when it was my turn she stood up and laughed at me, that's what really hurt. [Mimicking teacher's tone of voice] She said, "Well, you go to the office." I had a talk with the principal, and he say, "Reading? What's happening in reading?" and I say "I need some help in it." [Mimicking a condescending tone of voice] And he say, "Well you're supposed to be at this level, aren't you?" So we read again next day. Same thing. Couldn't get out of it. I started getting sick from that class.

SMOKEY: How long did it go on like that?

ROSE: For the whole year. But they passed me on to the 11th grade. But I didn't do anything, just there. I guess school didn't mean anything to me then, either, ever since I had such trouble in the 10th grade. In elementary school, I used to have good grades. I don't know what it was. Maybe because they explained it more or something. But I'd do my work and have a lot of C's to take home and my papers . . . I don't know I just didn't like school . . . I don't know I just didn't like school after that. I didn't never want to go back to school. But then my mother told me I ought to go back, and she was taking this real good English class [in a community college] she thought I would like, and I went to English class and my reading level was oh, 3.4 [3rd-grade, 4th-month level: that is, reading only short words]. I said, "Oh my goodness." I couldn't believe it but it was, it really was!

I had expected her written story to gain detail from its rehearsal in talk, but Rose's tale was far more elaborate in spoken than in written language. I spent quite a while comparing the transcript of our conversation with her written version of her story:

When I was in the tenth grade in English. The teacher did not even try to see if she could help, she would just tell me to read. I could not read very good and she would not show me how so she would send me to the office. I would go back to class so she told me to just sit, and watch for a hold year all I did was watch, so I did not come to school as much as I use to. And I did not like school any more.

I did not understand why so much of the color—the drama, the pizzazz—of Rose's speech was omitted from her writing. And, at least privately, I was a little embarrassed as well. I had thought her writing would gain *more* color, *more* detail, but what happened contradicted what I had blithely assumed would happen. Nonetheless, Rose was obviously making major progress toward competency in writing.

Rose continued to build her reading and writing skills. After a year or so of community college basic skills courses, Rose felt she had turned her life around. Her days of shyness before instructors were over, though she had a way to go before her writing met college standards and instructors' expectations.

I did not see her much after this, but I never forgot how proud she was to help her children with their schoolwork. She showed them her tests that "proved" she read "at 10th-grade level." She showed her children and she showed herself—but most of all she had evened the score with the teacher who had shamed her. As I look back, her story reminds me of something Mike Rose wrote in *Lives on the Boundary* (1989): Students like Rose seek to restore their education "not just [for] a few bucks more a week . . . ; literacy, here, is intimately connected with respect . . . the mastery of print revealing the deepest impulse to survive" (p. 216).

This fragment of one woman's learning was, for me, the trailhead—the point at which I stopped idly wondering about my students' histories and actively began to search for answers to questions that were still fuzzy. Though I did not know exactly what Rose's story could reveal about how talk and writing are related, I sensed its importance. It provided a local habitation and a name, a reason and a stronger impetus, for finding answers to my questions.

Why did someone like Rose, so anxious to learn and so able, arrive at a community college as a mature woman unable to read and write at what she called a 10th-grade level? I had a few ideas to go on. Rose felt deeply the disapproval of her teacher in high school; in college, she had gained confidence talking with teachers. This change in her relationships with teachers was central, I thought, to understanding her success. Having decided to find answers, I thought that the problems could be defined quickly and that I could get on with new and improved lesson plans. I was naive indeed.

In Theory: Educational Psychology Dominates

The professional journals I turned to offered answers, but, one by one, they were answers I had to refuse. As they put it, over and over, school failure was the result of the "Negro learner's" incompetence and was caused by genetic deficiency and aggravated by cultural deprivation. During the 1950s and well into the 1960s, proponents of the deficiency model dominated academic thinking about African American school failure.

Even the terminology used in the field of educational psychology in the 1950s and 1960s now sounds insulting. Terms such as "Negro," "incompetence," and "deficit"—which I use in this chapter to give the tone of this approach—should have led researchers to question the ethnocentric stance of those who laid down the theory. However, several years passed before a theoretical shift appeared, and with it came changes in nomenclature that signaled a new social and political awareness.

The language of deficiency showed up everywhere—in federal and state policies, in school administrations, in schoolrooms—and lingered long after researchers had rejected the deficit model. Youngsters coming from inner-city neighborhoods were assumed to be "deprived" by their heredity, their environment, and their culture. Because of academic test scores, and because many "Negro" families did not resemble the families represented in the primary-grade primers and readers, these researchers assumed such children were less able to master academic learning. These beliefs remained a powerful force in schools for years and had touched many of my adult students when they were children.

I realized then the power of a platitude I had never really thought about but never again forgot: Theories, not bits of evidence, shape conclusions. Hypotheses are formed by the light of what a researcher *believes* to be true; facts and situations can be interpreted to support these hypotheses, whether or not the underlying theories have been demonstrated.

It has been 40 years since I first read articles written from the deficit perspective. Educational research then was light-years behind where research on literacy is now. Then, the quantifiable research model ruled the social sciences and statistics ruled the interpretations. The countable, the observable, was placed at science's core. Educational psychologists, seeking to explain school failure among those they called "mentally deficient" and "culturally deprived," relied upon the statistical inferences they drew from low scores on IQ tests. These scores, they believed, demonstrated innate levels of intelligence. Researchers who identified some children as "White" and "middle-class" and others as "Negroes" noted that the White, middle-class youngsters typically had higher scores on these tests. Comparing these two groups, the researchers then pointed out what they saw as a significant contrast: Those learners whom they identified as "Negroes" frequently had lower IQ test scores. IQ test scores, offering what the deficit researchers saw as a scientific measure, provided the proof researchers like Arthur Jensen sought. Jensen titled his 1969 article in the *Harvard Educational Review,* "How Much Can We Boost IQ and Scholastic Achievement?" and answered his question by concluding, "Not much." In fact, he believed that "Negro" children could not benefit from an academic education and instead should be "trained" through some kind of rote memory technique for work that does not need high intelligence.

This dependence on IQ as an explanation of school failure still reemerges from time to time, as it did in 1994 when Richard Herrnstein and Charles Murray wrote *The Bell Curve: Intelligence and Class Structure in American Life.* But other researchers in the 1990s quickly pointed out the fallacies in that work. In the 1950s and 1960s, however, publications that opposed the view that minority children were deficient in intelligence—a view then held by a majority of scholars—were slow in appearing. For over a decade, the deficit view of minority groups' failure dominated the research field. Irving Gottesman (1968), Irwin Katz (1967), Arthur Jensen (1969), and Martin Deutsch (1967) formulated theories of deficit and, with their associates and doctoral students, undertook laboratory research. Carl Bereiter and S. Englemann (1966) consulted with schools to develop methods for applying deficit theory to classrooms. Many other researchers who followed them subscribed to some version of deficiency among those they called "disadvantaged." Educational psychologists debated vigorously, not whether deficiencies existed, but whether these deficiencies were the result of nature (genetic causes) or nurture (environmental influences).

The Genetic Inadequacy Model

There were two versions of the deficit theory. According to the genetic inadequacy model, Negroes were isolated from reproducing with members of the mainstream culture after their original "hybridization." Irving Gottesman (1968) wrote that Negroes were part of a "Mendelian breeding group" isolated from mainstream culture (p. 11) and that Negro children were members of this separate population.

The genetic inadequacy viewpoint extended few opportunities to those presumed to have school failure written in their DNA, but in spite of talk about genotype and phenotype, most of these researchers relied on appearance as criteria for identifying members of this separate population. Individuals were "more or less distinguishable on the basis of skin color, hair texture, and so on" (Katz, 1967, p. 255). Apparently, these "non-Caucasian" features locked Negroes into their living situations in groups that were "impermeable and separate" from the comings and goings of the larger culture.

Some researchers found that the "nurture" theory only strengthened the genetic argument: Poor school performance was linked with low intelligence, but low intelligence was what determined Negroes' fall into the lowest social class (Katz, 1967). As Jensen (1969) put it, Negro children fail at school because they are born with limited capacities. Their parents fail as providers for the same reason: Genetic predisposition and an inborn lack of ability determined Negroes' inevitable migration to the lowest income levels.

The Economic-Cultural Deprivation Model

Not everyone who explained the school failure of minority youngsters relied primarily on the genetic deficit argument. Some emphasized cultural deprivation, and Martin Deutsch was a central spokesperson for this position. In *The Disadvantaged Child* (1967), a volume reporting Martin Deutsch's experimental studies, he describes "experiential poverty" as placing a ceiling on the development of some children, a ceiling resulting from a "minimal range of stimuli," a high "noise to signal" ratio, a poor sense of time management, no expectation of rewards for task completion, a lack of objects in the home, and little use of adults as information resources (pp. 41–47). Poverty of this sort, he argued, might be the root cause of Negro children's poor visual acuity, lack of auditory discrimination, short attention span, and inadequate task completion—all central problems in the classroom. To test these hypotheses in detail, Deutsch performed a follow-up study that compared a poverty-stricken Negro school with a middle-class White school to demonstrate that specific environmental factors lead to poverty-stricken Negro children's cognitive and linguistic deficits (1967, pp. 90–131).

Researchers who subscribed to the economic-cultural deprivation model believed that minority children grew up with no objects to classify or label, and heard only poorly structured speech at home. The experts explained school failure in the light of these deficiencies. If these school-age youngsters lacked concept knowledge (Ausubel, 1964), inevitably they also lacked the words for discussing these concepts. If they lacked sentence complexity, then inevitably they were limited to a "non-logical mode of expressive behavior" (Bereiter & Engelmann, 1966, p. 113). Such findings led to statements like the following: that "[deprived children] truly have less language than other children" (Frazier, 1964, p. 70), and that "[teachers should proceed] as if the children had no language at all" (Bereiter & Engelmann, 1966, p. 113).

Basic Assumptions of Language and Culture

Ideas like these never just pop up out of nowhere; they always have roots. Where did the deficit theory come from? It emerged in the mid-20th century from ideas prevalent at the time among educational psychologists—ideas about intelligence, culture, and language.

Beginning before World War II, IQ was the primary measure of intelligence. IQ test scores were a major source of the future labels test takers would carry around with them, such as "smart" or "retarded." These scores also helped open the door to opportunity. The IQ tests measured performance in a testing situation that involved written language, and few, if any, researchers questioned whether such a "global ability"—called the g factor for "general intelligence"—existed. Those who scored at the bottom of the bell curve were viewed as inferior to those who scored in the middle or near the top. The deficit theorists' notions of intelligence were obviously linked with the field of psychology.

Educational psychologists turned to the stimulus-response model of language and language learning—that is, to what has been called the Pavlovian model—as a framework for language learning and learning in general. B. F. Skinner (1967) was a major figure in the behaviorist discussions of the 1950s and 1960s, grounding his work in the idea that "the study of human thought [was] the study of behavior" (p. 140). Skinner sought to understand thought through verbal behavior; he called language the "visible link" between the observable and the mental (p. 132). By identifying a few external stimuli in the laboratory, he believed he could predict verbal behavior accurately.

The deficit psychologists followed Skinner in assuming that "humans, like all mammals, possess the neural structures for . . . acquiring S-R [stimulus-response] habits" (Jensen, 1973, p. 132). As Jensen explains it, this capacity, according to Skinnerian mediation theory, is based on the acquisition of verbal mediators—that is, the "covert verbal responses [i.e., thoughts] to external stimulus which, in turn, act as stimulus for other responses" (p. 137).

While children learn in part through IQ-related "growth readiness," the most important component for learning is the child's prior experience with inputs of stimulus-response learning. As Jensen wrote in "Social Class and Verbal Learning" (1968), language develops through reinforcement of the infant's early vocalization efforts by certain kinds of responses. This reinforcement is necessary for language to develop into speech.

Deficit theorists adopted Skinner's assumptions and proceeded as if Negro children lacked both growth readiness and "covert" verbal training (or the ability to think). Deficit theorists believed Negro children did not, would not, could not become logical thinkers. Many educational psychologists of the time shared these ideas about intelligence, language, and learning. The sources of their notions about culture, however, were more difficult to find. After a search with dozens of dead ends, my readings on race and culture finally led me to connect the way some anthropologists defined primitive tribal units and the way deficit theorists defined what they called the "Negro" population.

I located a study published in 1964 in *Current Anthropology* by an anthropologist named Raoul Naroll. Like others in his field in the 1950s and 1960s, he sought to improve the cross-cultural research by determining "exactly where is the *skin* of a culture?" (italics in original; Ralph Gerard, quoted in Naroll, 1964, p. 283). Naroll detailed certain features of a *"cult unit,"* which he defined as "people who are domestic speakers of a common distinct language and who belong to the same state or the same contact group," factors he claimed identified "an operating social unit" (p. 286–287). He saw culture as a "skin," a sack with various factors isolating those inside from other cultures. Like the deficit theorists, he presumed this cult unit was identifiable by racial, territorial, and linguistic distinctions.

Anthropologists did not apply this framework to groups in the United States, yet educational psychologists assumed some notion of a bounded, impermeable group as they defined the sample of children they used to represent the Negro population.

I disagreed mightily with the deficit thinkers' conclusions and opinions, with their outmoded assumptions. I was angered by such comments as "Negro infants are not raised in a typical White infant's natural habitat, which includes adequate diet, two-parent home care, and . . . compulsory education" (Gottesman, 1968, p. 34). Yet, I had to accept the truth of what Clifford Hill (1977) at Teachers College, Columbia University, had said in a review. Despite what Hill saw as its wrong-headedness, he acknowledged that "the deficit position had more effect on public education than any other theory" (p. 1).

I did more than disagree with the conclusions of the deficit thinkers; I fumed in outrage. But my personal reactions only made me more inarticulate. I turned from these gut-level reactions to an analysis of these researchers' basic assumptions. I made an effort to understand their arguments rather than giving in to emotional outbursts against these ideas that denigrated almost every person I had taught for several years.

In Response: The Deficit Theories Weaken

Critics like Clifford Hill, Courtney Cazden, and William Labov—all of whom strongly rejected deficit models—found problems with almost every phase of the deficit theorists' work, from experimental design to conclusions (Cazden, 1972; Hill, 1977; Labov, 1972a). With regard to intelligence, most critics of deficit theory agreed that a single academic or IQ test was an inadequate measure of intelligence, particularly since such tests were biased in favor of middle-class children and were usually administered in the form of written examinations. From the beginning of their discussions about school failure, the deficit theorists connected intelligence to literacy. Psychologists Michael Cole and Jerome Bruner (1971) cautioned against this untested assumption. They pointed out that it had not been demonstrated that members of any one group were innately either more or less intelligent than members of any other group (p. 868). Yet the link between "smart" and "literate," "dumb" and "illiterate," still has not been broken.

Critics of Raoul Naroll's cult unit theory dismissed the claim that a cultural minority subgroup was able to remain distinct from other nearby cultural groups—that its social organization could be so neatly bounded. The concept of a tightly circumscribed Negro population was a cornerstone of the deficit argument, but even in 1970 the idea of defining culture in this way was criticized (Barth, 1998, pp. 5–7, 9–38). Further, the cult unit could not be applied to American society. White and Negro citizens shared many institutions, from health care to the legal system to education. The boundaries separating ethnic and cultural groups were permeable. Members of these groups, no matter how separated they may have been earlier in American history, were no longer distinct.

The deficit frameworks associated with intelligence and cultural separations were clearly based on outmoded theories. In a similar way, so were the theories associated with language. Skinner's language model was explicitly dismantled early in the 1960s. In 1959, Noam Chomsky constructed one of the early (and best) arguments against the Skinnerian or "operant conditioning" view of language. The general point of view of the behaviorist, Chomsky (1967) believed, was "largely mythology." Chomsky rejected the notion that the only important behavior was visible behavior, and said that Skinner's "astonishing claims are far from justified" (p. 142). Skinner's view of what could be performed in a laboratory both oversimplified the problem of input or stimulus and denied the contribution of the organism in response. In fact, Chomsky argued, language learning is accomplished by learners "independently of intelligence and in a comparable way by all children"—and sometimes, as in immigrant homes, without any parental input at all toward the child's growing development of the new language (pp. 170–177). Chomsky's "generative grammar"— so called because it attempts to outline how speakers generate sentences taken as "correct" in their cultural group—soon replaced the Skinnerian theory of language in many countries around the globe.

The Aftermath: Deficit Theories Linger

The deficit model's arguments now seem so clear—and so wrong. Once they were seen as lacking defensible assumptions, the arguments for deficit theory disintegrated and lost much of their power—even the power to make me angry. Yet many damaging labels applied to minority children in the schools today can be traced to influences from the deficit models of the past. That particular school failure battle was fought in the previous generation. Yet, a recent national survey on teachers' attitudes toward minority language varieties (Smitherman & Villanueva, 2003) suggests that the policy statement of 1974 called "Students' Right to Their Own Language" no longer accurately describes teachers' current attitudes.

In the 1960s, 1970s, and even the 1980s, teachers were caught in a hard place. With deficit thinking as the prevailing model, experimental studies "discovered" problematic cognitive and linguistic behaviors and began making restrictive classroom prescriptions. Teachers wanted to feel successful with their students and wanted their students to learn. What were these teachers to think when university researchers concurred with stereotypes already part of conventional wisdom? They were told that some children had no language. They were told to expect some children to fail. Researchers offered the teachers little to prevent this failure; in fact, the researchers provided reasons why teachers might expect it.

Perhaps Rose had been taught, as many Negro children were at the time, in programs designed to "teach these children English," programs in which she learned little about reading. Perhaps her teachers followed the advice of psychologists like Bereiter and Engelmann (1966) who advised, "Proceed as if the children had no language at all" (p. 111). Such advice made teachers feel that they needed to follow the structured lessons that came out of this period, lessons designed to teach learners "logical forms" needed for written language, such as "The book is on the table," as replacements for their "illogical forms" of spoken language, such as "There the book."

Perhaps teachers believed such English lessons helped. Perhaps they had already bought into the stereotype that said children whose skin was not White and whose hair was not straight could not learn. But change was in the air. The term "Negro" began to fall into disfavor among researchers and was replaced in most publications by the word "Black." In 1970, for example, Louisa Lewis concluded that teachers' low expectations for "Black learners" (p. 9) may be at the heart of the children's school failure. Whatever the explanation, in many schools, Rose and thousands like her simply got passed on or placed in Special Education classes where they learned little.

Even in the early 1960s, not everyone accepted the prevailing ideas of deficit theorists. Inspiring classroom narratives, like Herbert Kohl's *Thirty-Six Children* (1967), suggested that schools cared little for the children of color they taught. Daniel Fader in *The Naked Children* (1972) also described bright and knowledgeable youngsters in his classrooms. But these empathetic portraits of students were no antidote for (supposedly) scientific findings. In this period, classroom teachers did not consider asking their own questions or undertaking classroom research.

In Retrospect: The Legacy of Deficit Theories

My response to the deficit perspective was both personal and reasoned. After all, these researchers' assumptions and their answers did not fit my ideas about teaching, and they did not fit the students I knew best. What about Rose, who was capable as an adult, and no doubt as a child, but silent and ashamed when she walked into a classroom? Was I to believe that Rose, and hundreds like her, had too little g factor or IQ, to learn to read and write? This was a tale too tall to swallow.

By the end of the 1960s—despite all the research I have mentioned (and more besides), despite all the money spent on labs and special training equipment and all those pages of scholarly articles—little or nothing remained except the stigma that the work bequeathed. Most researchers put the deficiency models behind them and sought new explanations for the problems children of color faced in school. Most classroom teachers were left with few new ideas of how better to educate the large numbers of children who were their charges.

And I, a classroom teacher who had thought answers were easy to find, learned an important lesson: Almost no large questions have easy solutions—or single, simple answers.

Chapter 2

Mark:
Repeating School Failure

Why don't Mark and his teacher overcome earlier school patterns of failure?

In Practice

Many outcomes were not as satisfying as Rose's. From those earliest days, two other students remain in my mind: Mark and Kelly. With both, the school and I were unable to fulfill the promise of a second chance at education. Even with my rule of thumb–"Try 232 different approaches before you give up"—I did not know what to make of either of them, but for different reasons. Both students had been written off the public school ledgers; they had learned much from experience but much less from academic studies. Kelly, the student in Chapter 3, wrote a personal narrative fluently in about 15 minutes once he finally put pen to paper, but he left school before the semester's end. In contrast, Mark, the student in this chapter, had almost no skills. He could copy what I wrote, he told me, but he wanted to learn to write "cursive."

Mark came, I believe, from West Oakland. I could find out little or nothing about his home or school life. Was Mark living at or below poverty level? I did not know. Although all California residents aged 17 and older could attend community college, most of the students I saw were nearer to 27 years old. When Mark appeared in my basic writing course, his youth made him stand out. He could not have been more than 18, his youth emphasized by narrow shoulders and hips and a creamy clear complexion with no hint of beard or stubble. He had come to our community college from a "continuation high school," a citywide school where the district sent students whose history in neighborhood schools was marred by ongoing behavior or truancy problems. His former principal advised me to teach Mark as he was and not worry about his earlier situations.

Mark's behavior in my class repeated previous habits. He wandered into class and out again, and unless I sat with him, talked to him, and prodded him to copy what I had scribed for him, he mostly stared into space. A more experienced hand might have ignored him; even I, 10 years later, might have. But I did not, and he remains one of the students I remember really trying to listen to. The unfortunate part is that trying to listen was not enough. For me, he complicated the questions I sought to pin down. Why did Mark repeat old school behaviors—habitual absence, tardiness, and a lack of focus—while other students changed their school performance?

After several days of staring at his blank notebook pages, he told me he could not write "out of his own head." I suggested we tape-record what he wanted to tell about. Then he could listen to what he said and write what was on the tape.

I was not familiar with his style of storytelling, or with the experiences he described. Sometimes he said only a word or two; other times he talked endlessly. On the days he and I worked together, I kept trying to knead his interminable talk into a shape I knew. I suggested he tell about one scene at a time, fitting these episodes into what happened first, second, and so on—just as a television show has several scenes. As I re-read the transcript now, I notice my repeated mention of "scenes" and his puzzled "Huh?"

Over the course of about two weeks, Mark told several installments on the theme of "the man in the yella Baratz" (also, from time to time, referred to as the "big yella barrette"). Transcripts from the 2 weeks ran to more than 15 pages. The three segments provided here illustrate the troubles we shared.

The first excerpt from our conversation begins with my prompt for details about a car Mark mentions, and ends in Mark's silence. The variations in spelling illustrate the variations in pronunciation—mine because I can't understand him and his because he is trying to describe (I learn later) a Cadillac Biarritz. (The turns of the conversation are numbered so that specific moments of the dialog can be referred to easily later on.)

1. SMOKEY: A big yellow Barrette. What kind of car is it?
2. MARK: A big yellow barrette. It's a big car. It's a barretts like uh El Dorada.
3. SMOKEY: Oh, they look like an El Dorada, but they're better? How come?
4. MARK: They just better.
[Silence for 11 seconds]
5. SMOKEY: OK, ready? OK. What's the next important thing, the next scene?

The second segment illustrates Mark's response to my search for a "scene"—that is, a narrative—as I probed for an event and for the details that bring narratives into focus. As I pursued my conversational goal, I often interrupted him. Thus, my comments are placed in the midst of his sentences.

6. MARK: Uh. Then we had. After we had made a money. After these two weeks. I mean after a week we had made about $500.00 so then we couldn't do nothing with 500 dollars so we just went shopping—
7. SMOKEY: uh huh . . .
8. MARK:—and bought us some clothes . . . then he had spent 250 and I had spent 250. And then we bought us some clothes.
9. SMOKEY: Well, what'd you get? Do you remember?
10. MARK: Nah. Just suits. Um ummmm.
11. SMOKEY: One suit?
12. MARK: Yeh he got one and some shirts and slacks and then—
13. SMOKEY: OK . . .
14. MARK:—an' then we went to find uh to find the big barrette, the big yellow barrette, the barrette, and we couldn't find it and then we were starved and then one day we seen it. Pulled up then he gave us some more money, 50 dollars—
15. SMOKEY: You'd seen who?
16. MARK: The barrette, the big yella barrette. He stopped and he pulled up and talked to us and gave us 50 dollars each and then we axed him, uh, told him, uh, wanted to use the car for a week so we can be like high. He let us use it for a week so we was badder'n he was for a week and we earned us enough money to buy us a little car in just a week. And we bought us a little car . . . my birthday was 3 days away and then on my 13th birthday we bought us a car.
17. SMOKEY: Nice birthday present.

The third portion of the exchange shows both of us losing patience. I was frustrated because I thought I almost had an "Our Car" story; he was out of patience as I repeatedly asked him to clarify one word. I felt my in-control persona, the teacher's mask, beginning to slip.

18. MARK: Uh huh. But it wasn't it was a little car about 500 dollars, a whoop ty.
19. SMOKEY: A what?
20. MARK: Whoop ty.

21. SMOKEY: What is it?
22. MARK: A car that's not in top condition.
23. SMOKEY: Say that word again. Hooty?
24. MARK: Whoop Tee.
25. SMOKEY: A car not in very good condition. OK.
26. MARK: So then we were riding high for about . . . 2 months or a 1 month (pause) but we didn't make us any much money in that long [inaudible words]. We was that young so first thing you know we gave up that car and we was back walkin and we had got down and out—
27. SMOKEY: OK. Now wait. Scene 6 is losing the car, huh?
28. MARK: Huh? What scene?

Together, we made most of the communication mistakes two people could make. He did not lack language; in fact he flooded me with talk, but his use of street slang mystified me. I did not know what he meant by "Barratz," a term that sounded sometimes like "barrette" and sometimes like "Bratz," so that at first I was unsure just how many cars he was talking about. Further, while I had heard the gossip about drug dealers and their runners, his rapid flow of talk, spoken softly and in a high falsetto, meant that I was never sure what he and the friend he mentions—never with any names of course—were doing with "the man in the car." I remember thinking that he was too young to be "into all that." Afterward, I wished I had said something about drugs, dealers, and runners (for, of course, he was not too young). Looking back, it was easy to see what I should have done, but in the moment I understood only part of what he said.

One of the most uncomfortable and recurring problems I had was the length of time that often elapsed between my questions and his answers. Six seconds, so it is said, is the maximum a speaker waits comfortably for a partner to respond. Pauses extending beyond a few seconds seem endless, and, in turns 1–5 of the first segment, Mark's 11 seconds of silence left me scurrying to restart the conversation again.

Years later, I happened to see on the back of a Cadillac the word *Biarritz*. Too late to help me follow Mark's point, I finally understood how strange it must have seemed to him that a teacher was asking "What kind of car was it?" when he had told me the model (Biarritz) and expected me to figure out the make (Cadillac). Further, at last I understood that he was emphasizing the highly successful status of the "mentor"—most likely a "drug dealer"—who had helped him and his friend. Multiple blind spots in my background knowledge kept me from building on his comments. In fact, the more I asked for details, the less communicative he became. The lengthy pause, the point at which the conversation bogged down completely, was an early danger signal hinting at difficulties to come.

The accumulation of many such clashes drove me from class tense, sweaty, and tired, feeling as if I had reached the end of a workout. His favored incidents lacked character and plot; they centered on cars and the two faceless, nameless boys walking, walking, walking. Any of several of these incidents he referred to might have been adequate for a page or so of text. As turns 6–17 show, I hoped he would elaborate on the shopping trip with $500.00. I pressured him to tell me what the two of them bought, but my questions elicited no detail. After each I signaled to him to come to a close, a finishing point. I hinted at a wrap-up: "Ah," I said again and again, "so that's the end of scene 6. Good."

After I had repeatedly mentioned "end of scene," I finally realized he and I had no real agreement about what I thought we were doing. To me, his task was relating a single event, or "scene," and my task was to write down accurately and legibly his spoken words so that he could practice writing by copying. I saw us as "working on the script" he had once mentioned he wanted to compose. As for what he thought we were doing, I will never know.

An illustration of what happens when questions are not helpful appears after several attempts at this "script" in turns 18–28. Again, the talk has to do with the same all-but-invisible characters and actions that served as his plot: that is, he and his friend's effort to locate and drive a car. I thought we had managed to locate an event that he could relate in half a page or so. This achievement disappeared, however, with my repeated questions about what "Hooty" (or rather "Whoopty") meant.

The man in the "yella car" bought him a car. That had the makings of an experience to write about. My questions about a "whooptie," however, stymied that: not surprising that our rapport had fallen to nearly zero. My "scene 6" comment overlaps and almost drowns out his "Huh?" Perhaps more than any other moment in our interaction, turns 18–28 showed me just how far off the shared page the two of us had drifted.

These difficult exchanges haunted me—and more so when the next week Mark would disappear from class for good. I had wasted a lot of class time, mine and his, and I gained little. One thing I did learn was that we had repeated Mark's earlier problems with school, the struggles that had originally gotten him placed in an alternative high school and finally expelled from public education. Of course, since there are not any rough drafts in teaching, neither he nor I had a chance to rewrite our scene. But I did not take it quietly.

My purpose was to understand what could help students like Mark and Rose write more easily. I assumed that conversations with teachers about reading or writing would help the students. Instead, while some students, like Rose, found college a place to master what she had missed, others, like Mark, repeated earlier patterns. What accounted for the difference?

The questions kept changing, and I longed for the point at which I would figure out what I was doing. Speculations were easy. Perhaps Mark was more unskilled than Rose had been when she entered. Perhaps Mark had another kind of problem, such as a learning difficulty, or maybe he was much too personally acquainted with the life of the streets and the drugs he mentioned. Perhaps gender made a difference. But looking beyond Mark at the larger-than-Mark picture, I realized that the good intentions of a "caring teacher" were not enough.

Was our failure the result of Mark's problems, my problems, or our mutual problems stemming from a lack of shared background? How did it happen? Why did it happen that Rose and Mark, two students from similar neighborhoods and perhaps similar experiences, could wind up on such different paths?

In Theory:
Psycho- and Sociolinguistics Take Center Stage

Mark and I were not on the same page (maybe not even in the same book). Why not? To be sure, he is an extreme example, but our interaction highlights where teachers and students can go wrong.

As the 1960s became the 1970s, I found a stream of research opposed to the deficit notion. These fields of study were committed to underlying assumptions unlike those used by deficit writers, methods of participant observation that went beyond, or around, the bell curve. Unlike the educational psychologists, social scientists placed the blame for school failure among minority groups not with the child but, instead, with mainstream culture's lack of tolerance for those who were different (Kochman, 1972). And the term "Negro" disappeared, replaced by the term "Black."

Studies: Different, Not Deficient

During the 1970s the study of Black language and culture as "different, not deficient" took center stage. In contrast to those who had supported a deficit position, writers who shared Abrahams and Troike's (1972) notions of a pluralistic society believed that, in spite of inequalities, no "hierarchical concept of social difference in anthropology" justified those inequities (Baratz & Baratz, 1972, p. 3).

Cultural relativism meant there was no such animal as an incomplete or inferior language or culture. In the "difference" view, as Richard Light (1972) pointed out, speakers of all ethnicities were seen as rich bearers of culture, and studies of their daily activities were expected to reveal new sociolinguistic principles concerning language variation.

Emphasis on Cultural Differences. Researchers took on the tasks of describing members of Black culture, concentrating on subcultural lifestyles most distinctly separate from those of the mainstream. They used participant observation methods and described, for example, street-corner men, "swingers," and gang members (Hannerz, 1969, Keiser, 1972). For some, this interest in Black folkways had implications for education. Researchers like Roger Abrahams and Geneva Gay (1972) argued that schools should utilize these resources of Black language and culture. Teachers, principals, and school boards did not heed this advice.

William Labov has contributed much to issues in public life in medical, legal, and educational settings. Working in Harlem for several years, William Labov and his colleagues, notably Clarence Robbins, explored various aspects of Black language and culture with an eye to possible effects on schooling. From this work, various explanations for cultural influences on school failure emerged, including the role that peer pressure plays in reading failure. Labov, Robbins, and others directed their work toward discrediting the deficit model, as it distorted mainstream perceptions of the abilities of youngsters "to whom life dealt mainly low cards" (Labov, 1972a, Dedication).

Using a variety of research methods, these researchers demonstrated that the deficit researchers' experimental methods and their lack of knowledge of linguistics and of fieldwork methods invalidated their studies. For example, in answer to the deficit researchers' charge of "monosyllabic children," Labov and his colleagues (1972a) showed that in informal and familiar settings, Black youngsters were not nearly as silent as they were in the experimental laboratory (p. 206).

Emphasis on Linguistic Differences. Labov looked at many social issues, but as a sociolinguist, he spent a majority of his time examining language differences. He noted that children in Harlem used a classic Black dialect that differed in various ways from Standard English. Applying primarily psycholinguistic analysis, Labov in several of his articles illustrates various phonological and grammatical differences between Black dialect and Standard English. One article, for example, discusses contraction rules (i.e., "they mine" in Black English Vernacular versus "they're mine" in Standard English), deletion rules (i.e., when the verb "to be" is obligatory), and pronoun usage (i.e., "Me got juice" in Black English Vernacular among children younger than eight, versus "I got juice" in Standard English). Labov's main point is that Black English is not illogical because of these language differences, as some deficit researchers had concluded.

Additional studies contributed to our understanding of the unique flavor of these speakers' communicative styles: of special vocabulary (Johnson,

1972); of semantic inversions such as "bad" meaning "good" (Holt, 1965; Mitchell-Kernan, 1974); of nonverbal dimensions of differences in greetings and eye-advertence patterns (Cooke, 1972); and call-response behaviors (A. Williams, 1972).

Taken together, all these studies showed that African-American children were not lacking in linguistic resources. Instead, these youngsters brought resources indigenous to their own culture to the classroom—resources that were "different" from mainstream styles. The schools erred, these researchers thought, in denying these children's linguistic strengths a legitimate place in schools.

The question remained: Did these language conflicts negatively influence classroom performance? With his background in African influences on the speech of American Blacks, William Stewart thought it likely. Stewart, like Labov, demonstrated grammatically significant differences between Standard English and Black dialects. It stood to reason, he argued, that speakers of Black English might have trouble learning to read Standard English (Stewart, 1972). Yet when pre-primers or primer texts using a "graduated" progression from Black English to Standard English were used with beginning readers, those in the experimental group did not read better than those children who used conventional Standard English–only primers (Melmed, 1973; Simons, 1979).

In spite of these findings, researchers continued to look for interferences that could clarify the sources of the problem that school presented to many Black learners. Researchers began to look at what happened in classrooms to find points of conflict (Piestrup, 1973). Furthermore, if there were these conflicts, how did they operate? In this view, dialect differences were not the sources of conflict, but rather the "symbols of conflict" (Labov, 1972a, xiv). Students in some schools equated academic success with "being a lame." Labov suggested that when researchers wanted to understand school failure, they would probably find that studying peer pressure was more useful than studying linguistic differences.

Basic Assumptions: Language and Culture

Sociologists and psychologists who stressed political, cultural, and linguistic differences as the cause of poor academic performance generally based their key assumptions upon perceived cultural and/or linguistic gaps. Those who focused on cultural differences between Black and mainstream societies maintained a view of the United States as a culturally pluralistic country—a world in which groups mix but do not combine. Instead of depicting America as a melting pot, they used the metaphors of a tossed salad or a vegetable stew.

One starting point for this view of America, so far as I could discover, came in 1944 near the end of World War II. J. S. Furnivall (1944), a social historian interested in colonization, examined the social structure of colonial empires in Africa during the 19th century. In these empires he found three groups: Caucasian colonizers, immigrant midmanagers, and native workers. These groups interacted in limited ways at places of employment like shipyards or coffee and cotton fields, or in the homes where natives worked as domestics. This colonialist model was transposed from Africa and India to the United States, leading to a view of the Black community as a unit separated from other units, or streams, of American life (Abrahams & Troike, 1972, p. 4).

An obvious next step for these researchers, then, was to examine communication among members of disparate groups: Do White teachers' ways of speaking, reading, writing, and thinking differ from the language styles of Black students? If differences create conflicts, what is the source of these differences?

One possible source, some researchers believed, was a linguistic difference. In this view, the origin of Black dialect was rooted in African languages and not in European English, leading to misunderstandings between speakers of Standard English and African American English Vernacular (or "Black English"). By comparing these two language varieties, dialectologists in fact did find that important features of American Negro speech had persisted from African languages of the slaves.

Raven and Virginia McDavid (1972), experts in the field of American dialects, compared the structures of Black dialect with structures of African languages and found many similarities. They cited Lorenzo Turner's studies of Africanisms in the Black English dialect called Gullah (or "Geechee"). This regional speech of Blacks along the South Carolina and Georgia Sea Island coast was shaped by African languages and by the pidginized English of the Caribbean (McDavid & McDavid, 1972, p. 217). William Stewart (1972) emphasized that modern Black English has retained features of non-European languages. At the time they were introduced, these findings provided evidence that the language of American Blacks had roots in the speech of the African Diaspora. This evidence strengthened the argument that the school failure of Black children is caused by communication conflicts.

Like dialectologists, other social scientists disputed the educational psychologists' deficit model as an explanation for Black learners' school failure. These researchers sought to show that Black English is not a deviant form of Standard English, as the deficit researchers had assumed, but instead is a full and complete language. One of these scientists, the linguist Noam Chomsky, saw the regularities in Black youngsters' speech and grammar as a demonstration of the children's linguistic competence. He argued that children generally mastered most of the forms of language they heard around them by the time they approached school age. Chomsky's idea of innate linguistic competence as every person's birthright became the prevailing view of language in the 1970s and influenced many "difference" researchers.

Anthropologists, too, rejected the assumptions of the deficit researchers, especially their determination to place Western Europeans' "ethnic heritages" at the center of the universe. Having studied cultures in every corner of the world, these anthropologists emphasized that no one culture or language was inherently better than another; no one language variety was more correct than the other. Cultural relativity—a belief that no one culture's is superior to another—had become a cornerstone of social science.

As these theoretical notions became widespread, researchers began to apply them to social issues like law and education. Dialect studies, psycholinguistics, and anthropology were all brought to bear on the problem of school failure for minority youngsters, particularly Black children.

Linguists interested in social issues (and thus called sociolinguists) explored differences between the structures of American Standard English and Black English. They reasoned that if the deep structures of Black English were African and not European, then of course there would be linguistic conflicts—and as a result, school problems—for Black learners in American classrooms.

This drawing together of theory and practice is notable in the remarks of the teacher trainer Richard Light. Referring to Chomsky's *Aspects of the Theory of Syntax* (1965) in one of his articles, Light (1972) cautioned against judging linguistically diverse speakers. He wrote that "regardless of cultural background, all normal children control the phonology and grammar of at least one language by age six" (pp. 14–15). Again, the implication is that in the case of Black dialect speakers, the language they hear as children will be Black English.

In the 1970s, education researchers explored several dimensions of the differences between mainstream and minority cultures. Their work was grounded in the best theory the disciplines had to offer. Psycholinguistic reasoning gave power to the arguments of those speaking against deficit notions. I cheered from the sidelines.

In Response: The Other Side of the Deficit Coin

The psycho- and sociolinguistic lines of research had opened up new areas for study. Each volume or article I read seemed to lead to three or four others on a must-read list. The flood of evidence that differences were not necessarily deficiencies silenced, in large part, the deficit researchers and weakened the deficit hypothesis.

Still, the difference investigations also made use of an outmoded view of culture and used ideas of linguistic differences to make some school-children seem exotic and "other." When cultural relativism was applied to American schools, it established a group clearly separate from the mainstream. While it could help teachers of Black students appreciate the verbal resources the children brought to school, it did little to help teachers close the performance gaps.

It seemed to me that the difference researchers made some of the same errors the deficit researchers had. The deficit researchers treated Whites and Blacks as completely separate populations, with those they called "Negroes" being deficient to those they called "Caucasians." The difference researchers rarely compared the two populations, but rather studied the group they called "Black" as being exotic and other. In the 1970s, "Black is beautiful" replaced most talk of "Negro" or "colored."

Yet in American daily life neither of these two groups was or is isolated from one another. White Americans and Black Americans shared many values, from religion to capitalism, from family values to respect for education. As a case in point, when teachers were persuaded to introduce reading via primers written in phonologically coded Black English Vernacular (BEV), Black children's parents protested mightily. Enraged families said they expected schools to teach their youngsters Standard English and not "hold them back" with what the parents saw as half-baked ideas. In fact, in the rush to change the school instead of the child, the difference researchers did not take into account the interweaving between Black and White cultures. Thus they did little to close the performance gap between Black and White students.

Like Naroll's cult unit, cultural pluralism emphasized what was inside a cultural boundary. In later research, as the next chapters show, anthropologists began looking at the seams between cultures, the boundaries between the mainstream and the "other" (Barth, 1998, pp. 5–7).

In Retrospect: Where Were the Teachers?

I read and searched through the many studies by those who had treated Black culture as unique, complete, and of value and learned much about Black English. Mark's and my conversations certainly confirmed difference in language varieties, and our talk provided ample evidence of linguistic interferences and cultural differences.

In the end, the cultural relativism had suggested very few (if any) strategies that helped resolve what went wrong between Mark and me. I had tried to shape his anecdotes into "scenes" like television scripts in an attempt to find a middle ground between my ideas of narrative needed for school and his picaresque tales about "the man in the yella Baratz." I did not succeed.

I did not want to push Mark out of school; quite the opposite. But what could I have done differently? Difference research provided findings and facts to work with, but it was up to me and to other teachers to figure out how to apply them.

Where were the voices of other teachers, those who could give me practical advice and maybe words of direction or comfort as well? There were few places for teachers to publish in the 1970s. Certainly very few teachers who intended to remain classroom teachers were publishing studies about their own classrooms. My questions got more complicated and less focused. I had to wonder not only about why some students succeed, but also about why others, who are similar to them in many ways, continue their old patterns of failure.

Part II

FINDING A FOCUS

The two chapters in Part II—"Kelly: Schooling as Irrelevant" and "Anthony: Transforming Talk Into Writing"—describe, as did Part I, two students whose college experiences ended quite differently—surprisingly so.

Kelly was an adequate writer, yet he did not complete one semester in college. Anthony was scarcely a writer when he began, yet he stayed in school for several semesters, and basic writing classes opened the floodgates of stories he wanted to tell, of worries about his family that he wanted to record.

Mark and Rose, Kelly and Anthony: similar students, different outcomes. As Part I emphasized, for more than a year it was not clear what direction my research might take. At last, however, a clear direction appeared: How do extended teacher/student conversations affect students' school performance? I might miss much by concentrating on classroom talk, but this tighter focus also meant that I had a greater chance of learning something specific.

As the "Guide" suggests, "Finding a Focus" is when the researcher realizes what kinds of situations and artifacts will form the center of the next project. Much remains unknown, but once the camera lens is trained on a single question—a single idea—the focus remains constant.

Chapter 3

—

Kelly:
Schooling as Irrelevant

"The saying of words . . . it's a love, a passion," says Toni Morrison.
Was Kelly afraid that schooling would take away his own "saying of
words"?

When I think of students like Rose who were successful as adults at catching literacy from their teachers, I cannot forget the ones who were not, like Mark and Kelly, for they fanned the flames of *why*. Their ghosts still haunt me, and what happened to Kelly was enough to wake anybody up in the night.

In Practice

I met Kelly when he came to the Writing Center and told me he was now going to get himself an education—with the kind of fervor that sounded like "Get an ed-u-CA-tion!" He must have been in his mid-twenties. He was well-dressed in a way no one I knew could match, and good-looking in the way that only those who look always in control can be. Outwardly calm, he looked like he knew it all already, no matter what the circumstances. I guess (in spite of his cool confidence) circumstances must have sometimes pushed him, for he occasionally dressed in suits to go to court or missed class to "take the girls to Fresno." I asked nothing and wanted to know even less about what he did when he left class.

I did, however, want to teach him to do well in school, for, however cool he looked, the fact was that his writing was not as sophisticated as his appearance. He told me he knew how to write, but he just did not get around to doing it.

If I ignored some visible facts of Kelly's life, they showed up in his work anyway, and it was his particular talk and text that led me to confront an unspoken, even unrecognized, conflict in cross-cultural expectations. One day a new draft appeared in his folder. His narrative (of which the ending is copied below) tells about a gambling game—most likely fictionalized, for I had read a very similar tale from two or three other students. In this writing, an innocent boy meets some older guys set up in the back of a bus.

LOSING THE GAME

> They said now let's play for money O.K. I agre to play for money than we agree to play for five dollars. Kowing that its going to be a sinch to win. I was so excited and fill with lots of happenness than we begin to play, he starded to mixing them up, and say a short poem, find the red card, you win, find the black card you lose my friend. The stragned thing he did was turn one black card over and then the other black card. And he told me to put my foot on the one I picked. I was posictive that I pic the right card, and I was excited. Knowing that I won. . . . Oboy, when I turn that black card over I though I would faint, how ironic it was when I lost. My head drop, my heart [pounded] so hard that I though I was going to have a heart attack. From that experience I promise to never and ever play that game as long as I live and that a promise.

From an academic's viewpoint, he had a good start, but it was definitely a first draft. Yet he did not want to change or add anything. His interest in writing began to falter in ways I had seen before with others. I wanted him to revise what he had written, but he wanted to talk to me to "explain" something. The next time I saw him, I again nudged him to revise, and he again wanted time to explain. We faced stalemate. Finally, we made arrangements for him to talk about, to "explain," his written work. We met during my office hours, with me still hoping I would be able to persuade him to concentrate on improving what he had written, or start writing something that "mattered" to him more.

We met near our classroom in a small area where instructors kept books and supplies. I remember setting the tape recorder between us on an ancient rug someone had brought from home. The storage room was not an inviting place, but it was private. He would not have sought me out in my assigned office across campus.

When he came in, we went through the usual greetings, and he pulled out a deck of cards. Though I wondered what I had gotten myself into, there was not much to do except say, "OK. Go." He changed posture, held the cards ready to deal, pitched his tone of voice into one I had not heard before, a falsetto whine, and struck up a double-time speech rhythm. In many ways, it reminded me of the performers in oral societies who—like

Homer among the Greeks, the *scop* of Celtic tradition, or the "teller" in African life—can reproduce lengthy poem-like narratives. Armed with a store of rhythmic phrases, these singers can extemporaneously create ballads to fit the themes and forms they know (Lord, 1960). In Kelly's performance, the performance foregrounds not only this verbal dexterity but his skill as a hustler; he is in control. Each time he mentions a face card or a number ("See that deuce? He's a bellhop"), he turns that card face up. This brief excerpt from the longer piece will give some of its flavor, but fails to capture the command he brings to the performance.

Mr. Bellhop

This is called Pimps Players and Hustlers, all right?
I was settin round the pad one day
Sittin all alone, had just moved into this big fine penthouse
I was up on about the eighteenth floor
[*turns up the two of diamonds*]
this deuce, look at that deuce.
That deuce was ba-aa-ad, was a ba-a-aa-d one.
Watch, he's a bellhop. So I said, Mr. Bellhop,
It's Friday night. Do you know anybody around?
Matter fact, I do. What you wanna do?
Play a poker hand if I can.
So what that bellhop did,
[*aside to listener: "cut . . . now put that card on top"*]
So what he did, he walk down one floor.
He walk down two floors, three floors, four floors, five floors . . .
So I said, who did you get me my man?
He said I got you the four King Brothers
[*turns up the kings of hearts, diamonds, clubs, and spades*]
So I said where you get them brothers at, and
He said between Sixth and Seventh Avenue.

This "I" is a fictionalized character who, by using the services of Mr. Bellhop, goes on grand adventures—each card appearing as a part of the setting or as one of the characters engaged in escorting a stranger around a strange town.

The delivery is smooth and composed of formulaic phrases that allowed rapid delivery. This performance, what he called a story, was (he told me later) a lead-in to a card game called Three Card Molly. I had heard of the game. I had read about it as Three Card Monte in England and had watched parents, principals, and policemen trying to stop it on campus or on the street corner. I had never seen it performed by a master.

Thinking about it afterwards, I put Kelly's writing together with that polished spoken piece. The written form (lacking the niceties of spelling and punctuation) satisfied the letter, if not the spirit, of the instructor's assignment. In contrast, the spoken form, the oral performance, mattered a great deal to Kelly.

Toni Morrison says that what makes her fiction distinctive is "the saying of words . . . it's a love, a passion." I saw Kelly through Toni Morrison's eyes when she said, the "worst of all possible things . . . would be to lose that language" (quoted by LeClair, 1981, p. 27).

I still think of Kelly there at the height of his youthful confidence: He seemed determined to have it all. School writing, I thought, could offer him and those like him new knowledge. Writing could open an avenue to language use he had not explored but, at the same time, not close off his verbal repertoire.

But I was troubled and puzzled. Kelly had the ability and the skill but it became clear that he could not place himself in a "one-down" position, as correcting writing mistakes apparently was for him. Why did he not care more? Why could he not become involved in revisioning his composition? Kelly was half in and half out of class for the rest of the semester, but I always knew he was not engaged and that I had taught him little, or nothing at all.

Some mornings I woke up questioning the kind of work I was doing with students like Rose, Mark, and Kelly. At other times, I resolved to understand the puzzle instead of wringing my mental hands. Here it was, face-to-face: the cultural divide. Where did academic learning fit into lives like Kelly's? I knew it *could* fit, but I needed to give much more weight to differences than I had. I needed to learn more about other value systems and kinds of culture. And yet, of those who decide to "get an education," some—in fact, many—find various kinds of success at college. Difference theory alone was not enough to explain why the chasm between home and school could be sometimes narrow, and other times almost unbridgeable.

IN THEORY:
MACROSTRUCTURAL APPROACHES APPEAR

My research focus sharpened. Why did school help some students turn their lives around while it remained irrelevant or full of conflicts for others? I sought answers from those who explained cross-cultural clashes between schools and students as part of America's social organization. This "big picture" view came to be called the macrostructural approach.

During the 1970s, almost nothing more was heard from deficit theorists. Difference theorists who had studied Black culture as customs of "the others" began looking at such differences in terms of their effects on education. A new wave of thinkers, some anthropologists and some social critics, began to write about schools as oppressive, nonfunctional, and conflict-filled spaces. They reasoned that home and community shape language and culture, and that schools socialize differently those children who are not part of mainstream America. In this view, schools, as major sites of conflict, contribute to social dysfunction. A central theme of research during the mid- and late 1970s focused on the effects of race, class, and caste on schooling.

Class-Based Views

Following Marxist-influenced theories, Samuel Bowles and Howard Gintis, two economists, presented a watershed study from the conflict perspective in *Schooling in Capitalist America* (1976). Noting that the U.S. educational system was failing to achieve its goals of educating all of America's children equitably, they argued that schools were socializing learners to fit into the hierarchical structure of modern corporations. Those at the bottom of the schooling hierarchy—the poor and members of historically distinct populations of color—were treated in school as they would be by corporations should they seek white-collar jobs. They lagged behind their wealthier White peers in the development of cognitive abilities, linguistic possibilities, and economic parity. These inequities were passed from generation to generation.

Conflict- and Resistance-Based Views

Unlike the economists, Paolo Freire stood outside the formal United States educational system. Yet he also wrote from the perspective of conflict and resistance. Even before his *Pedagogy of the Oppressed* (1970; 2000) was translated into English, Freire's work was well known and was referenced in many publications as a philosophy successful with uneducated adults. Freire offered content relevant to the lives of Brazilian workers. His work inspired an entire generation—though I had not even the vaguest idea how to translate his rural pedagogy of "read the word to read the world" into an urban milieu. In principle, it seemed simple: When people acquire the tools to read and write they arrive at a new sense of their own

condition; their lives change; and they can better determine their own futures. Freire's work influenced American education through its focus on
issues of social justice. This work embodied the "education for life" that
many studying in graduate schools during the 1970s and 1980s hoped to
find in American schools.

When researchers turned to urban American classrooms, they were
disappointed. The progressive ideas they had absorbed were absent, and
study after study reported business as usual: dismal findings for the Black
underclass. Some children were not learning to learn, it was said, but were
learning to fail, while others were developing new cognitive abilities and
academic language with which to succeed. Often the studies implied that
teachers promoted these inequities. Following the lead of *Schooling in
Capitalist America* (Bowles & Gintis, 1976), some researchers attacked the
inequity in classrooms as parallel to the society-wide inequalities of job-
lessness and prejudice.

Social sciences had moved past the simplistic lines that deficit thinkers had drawn between races and cultures to explain school failure. Applying frames for analysis unlike those that Jensen and others had used,
anthropologists and sociologists were focusing attention on urban life in
all its complications.

For some researchers in these areas, race became less and less a description of an external reality and more a political and cultural artifact.
Rather than studying groups of people as naturally, inevitably separate, researchers began examining settings and situations in communities where
institutions were utilized by members of historically distinct ethnic and
social backgrounds who by law were guaranteed equality but by social
convention had been denied equal access.

With many differences identified, diversity became undeniable. Nevertheless, even though many social groups were all served by the same
public schools, boundaries still existed. Perceiving society as unequal re-
sulted in researchers criticizing schooling for its failure to meet both the
letter and the spirit of the laws demanding equity.

It was not new to read volumes of research that were critical of schools.
Abrahams, Labov, and Kochman (see Chapter 2), seeking to put African
American community folkways and speech on the map, had also been
critical. Yet there was a new bitterness in the tone of the criticism. After a
year of participant observation in primary schools, Ray Rist (1973) charac-
terized the school as a "factory for failure." Several researchers used images of combat; they spoke of the containment of Black culture through daily
warfare between White teachers and Black students. Arguments ran like
this: Institutional bureaucracy held the power to co-opt teachers, to force
approval of a watered-down curriculum, and thereby to limit educational

opportunities. These limits, it was argued, purposely prepared youngsters to function only within their own community (Levy, 1970; Stein, 1971).

The Cultural-Stereotype View

Among studies that viewed classrooms as mirrors of larger social institutions, a few examined teacher attitude. Social psychologists assumed that stereotypes and prejudices frequently exist below the threshold of awareness. It follows, they said, that teachers' negative attitudes about members of a particular ethnic group or social class are unconscious. They can be triggered by the others' appearance, speech, or behavior. Such cultural stereotypes are products of unconscious or institutionalized racism and lead to differential treatment.

Using an experimental method called the "matched guise" technique, experimenters have observed subjects making evaluations about others' personality, ethnicity, intelligence, congeniality, and appearance by how they speak. For example, if a bilingual individual is tape-recorded speaking Spanish in one text and English in another, and listeners rate this speaker as "gentle" when listening to the English version and "violent" in the Spanish-speaking one, a *cultural stereotype* is said to be at the root of the differential judgments (Lambert, Hodgson, Gardener, & Filenbaum, 1960).

Using this approach, Frederick Williams (1970) hypothesized that teachers judged speakers on the basis of ethnicity and social status. Schoolchildren whose language was marked by features of African American speech, Williams found, correlated with judgments of "lower class." This line of research also showed that teachers of African American background rated speakers differently than did those teachers who were White (Naremore, 1971).

Caste-Based Views

Criticism of the conflict between the schools and the Black underclass was bitter. John Ogbu took a more deterministic position. His model of ecological adaptation saw the American social structure as a system of highly specialized niches that groups were slotted into by facts of birth and class and to which each group adapted to maintain the ecological balance. He became a widely known spokesperson for those of minority descent who were "unwilling immigrants" and who had adapted generation after generation to the low-paying mainstream jobs America offered them. Ogbu (1978) called groups brought to the United States against their will "caste-like minorities" (p. 351). Applying ethnographic methods, he focused not on the meetings of particular children in particular classrooms but on education as a way to prepare children of color to adapt to the economic and social limitations that would be placed upon them (p. 213). Historically locked in stasis, the conflict between schools and Black Americans maintains the status quo and maintains America's stratified society.

When one looks at society, it is possible either to concentrate on particular students and teachers—the trees—or else to see the big picture—the forest. John Ogbu held the second view, which came to be called the *macro-structural approach*. He wanted to know why only certain kinds of minority children failed in school.

Caste-like minorities fail in school, Ogbu (1978) argued in his study of minority education, as part of an overarching adaptation to what will be "their inferior social and technoeconomic positions in adult life" (p. 228). In light of job ceilings, they perceive that school does not provide the equal opportunity it promises. In *The Next Generation: Ethnography of Education in an Urban Neighborhood* (1974), Ogbu describes communities of people who live in a low-income area in a midsized city. He explained the high rate of school failure among African Americans and Mexican Americans in this locale as "both a reaction and an adaptation to the limited opportunity available to them to benefit from their education" (p. 12). Ogbu called his systems approach *adaptive cultural ecology*. In an undated manuscript titled *The Origins of Human Competence*, he explained how socialization operated to produce differential performance by minority children. Education, he reminded us, fills the roles or cultural tasks families expect; subsistence—making a living—is one measurement of meeting social expectations.

Ogbu pointed out that most researchers have looked only at the middle-class values of earning power and social power as a measuring stick for school failure, not at the dual system of social mobility under which caste-like minorities live. The value systems of both mainstream and minority communities influence child-rearing practices. During socialization, minority youngsters' competences and values are shaped at home, at school, and, for some, on the street. These three socialization influences develop "types" and competences.

Cultural demands, Ogbu (1978) stated, develop specific cognitive skills. In school, the "flight from learning" is adaptive, "*a part of the training of black children for their survival*" (p. 199, italics in original). Kelly, I believe, developed his competences from street influences. In his hustler's performance, Kelly demonstrates an adaptation to one of the avenues of success open to those who participate in the alternative urban economy.

Does an "ecological" analysis of America's social structure explain how Kelly could both want an education and not want one? Knowing he is successful in one environment, might it be too risky, too late, or too much work to seek mainstream success on an academic track? Whatever his individual reasons for his choice, a macrostructural explanation helps us see Kelly as an adult who already had a broad repertoire of competences. As I thought carefully about Ogbu's arguments, I wondered how—and if—individuals choose one set of values over the other.

In Response: The Social System View

I found it hard to accept that teachers are merely preparing their pupils to fill positions as domestic workers and janitors, as Ray Rist, Annie Stein, Ray McDermott (1976), and others said. Nevertheless, those studies pointed out, rightly, many of education's shortcomings and problematic practices. But do we understand enough to assume that the education system *intended* to do its worst for large groups of students? The class-based argument offered no way to explain the many successful minority, low-income students who would have to be regarded as exceptions to the rule. The adaptive culture line of reasoning, however, did suggest a way of fitting findings of school failure and success into all-encompassing cultural practices—interrelating cognitive, social, and economic practices.

Ogbu's work described a range of life choices under what he called the native theory of "making it." A habitual "mental withdrawal from schoolwork" could have been the result of a student's recognition of "limited future chances for opportunities" (1978, p. 237). No wonder, then, that in place of the "lower social and occupational positions in adult life" to which caste-like minorities were restricted, Kelly chose to adopt work that risked much but carried possible wealth and status among segments in the Black community. Though Kelly's choices of employment did not show up on the government's lists of employment categories, he hoped that his charisma as an entertainer, pimp, and hustler would provide for him.

Ogbu's broad macrostructural interpretation has been an important and widely recognized explanation of school performance. His interpretations have various applications. For example, he describes certain employment roles available to adults in the Black community, including the Workingman, the Client, the Reformer, the Entertainer-Hustler, and the Street Man. Like Marxist interpretations, these labels take away individual identities in exchange for a broad brush, sounding very much like the harshest of stereotypes. Are these the "adult economic roles" teachers and schools should prepare youngsters and adolescents to take on? If these are the realities, as Ogbu suggests, then what relevance can school have for minority learners?

Did Ogbu's macrostructural view mean social change was impossible? Would we always separate the mainstream elite from everyone else and live in divided and partly segregated communities? It may be so. But if this deterministic view explained school failure, was there no theoretical way to understand how societies change? Much about cultural adaptation worried me. But most of all, I was concerned that Ogbu's theoretical answer removed the possibility of change from specific individuals. He places the mechanics of social change entirely in the hands of large-scale policies, acknowledging that individual successes are not his primary focus. Yet, for teachers each success must be central. In his view, individual change comes only after macrostructural change. "The elimination of past academic barriers . . ." he tells us, requires the "creation of a new social order" (1978, pp. 357–360). But if we must change society before we can change lives, this generation—and the next, and the next—should just give up.

Change does not only trickle down. Change at individual and group levels can also "trickle up" and affect policy. If we seek social change, transformation at the microstructural level is no more utopian than the macrostructural demand for complete systemic overhauls before change can begin. In the end, the theory of cultural adaptation offered no way to explain individual transformation and lasting social change.

So long as the law provides equal opportunities and public rhetoric speaks about these opportunities, barriers can be overcome. If individuals shape society as much as society shapes us, then it is worth finding a theoretical answer to the breakthroughs and successes. A social theory needs to build in an avenue for change. The destruction of job ceilings as sole remedy to educational problems seems both unrealistic and much too simple, but of course it might be part of a scenario that leads toward remedy. Although Kelly and Mark were repeating their old school habits, students like Rose—from the same neighborhoods, with similar schooling history—were changing theirs. Rose had used education to obtain what she wanted—not only a victory over that high school teacher who told her she could not read at a "10th-grade level," but new competences, along with the completion of her AA degree and job-training certification, new aid for her children, and a new sense of respect from family and friends.

No matter how important equal access to employment is, so much more could be responsible for school failure than employment barriers, and much more could be responsible for school success than the promise of a good job. Gender could be central, new self-images could be central, new beliefs and motivations could be central—and what went on in the classroom, I thought, could be central as well.

This book assumes alternate paths by which we can understand school failure and, more important, school success. Rather than examining the macrostructural view, as Ogbu did, the studies in this book describe what happens in classrooms, at the microstructural level between teacher and student.

On that border between childhood patterns of school failure and adult patterns of school success, the interactions that make a difference can help explain social change. We can learn from studies like these how it is that some students move past gates closed for too long.

Whatever else it might have been, Kelly's speech to "go with the story" was (by my lights) neither a story nor an explanation—both labels he claimed for the patter that prepared the audience to play Three Card Molly. For me, it was instead a window on a life that was totally out of my middle-class and academic experience, and a life he seemed unwilling to forego. Or, to put it differently, he seemed unwilling or unable to add an academic style to the charismatic style that served him so well in his community.

In Retrospect: Finding Teachers' Voices

Kelly was perhaps 25. It is hard to change one's lifestyle at that point. Yet there are many who do manage to change their paths; I have seen them and describe some of them in this book. Moreover, many youngsters in school are ready to back off from what may seem as preordained lifestyles. What might have happened if the school had been more ready to listen to Kelly and to engage in dialog with him about his life choices? Maybe someone did eventually—his mother, a teacher—who knows? My point is that students can change if they and school come together at a moment when both are ready to listen to each other, and for that to happen students need teachers.

In more than 30 years of teaching, I have witnessed too many transformations to believe in mere exceptions. I learned a useful dimension from Ogbu and his colleagues, but their theories did not explain why some students of minority status make it and others do not. So the question re-emerges: What *happens* in a classroom to help one student succeed where others fail?

I was lucky that research appearing in the 1980s considered the same question. Shirley Brice Heath's early publications, such as "What No Bedtime Story Means," became a part of her ethnographical study of individuals within three communities. This work, *Ways with Words* (1983), describes how cultural and linguistic practices in three communities in the Piedmont of the Carolinas influenced school performance.

But in all my studies, something nagged in the back of my mind; something was missing, something about the way the studies were being set up, something that felt off. Then I realized what was missing. In the studies I had been reading, teachers' voices were still muted or absent, and with them the voices of their students.

This was about to change. Mina Shaughnessy brought the language of open-admission students from the City College of New York to the page when she published *Errors and Expectations* in 1977. There was no more influential teacher during those decades when teachers were meeting students unfamiliar with academic ways. But her emphasis was on the conflicts between the varieties of language these students wrote on their initial placement exams and the language teachers expected. In spite of her work, the voices of teachers describing their classrooms had barely begun to appear. In general, teachers went on being ignored or being treated with condescension by the research world. Without hearing from those most involved, we have no way to understand how global social issues can be worked out in local settings.

Chapter 4

—

Anthony: Transforming Talk Into Writing

*Why does my acknowledgment of a misunderstanding repair a commu-
nication breakdown with one student? What promise did this interaction hold for transforming talk into writing?*

In Practice

By the fall of 1978, after what seemed at the time an eternity, I had a hand-
ful of students' writing and transcripts of talks with them. With some, like
Rose, the communication had been unremarkable. With others, like Mark
and Kelly, interactions had been strange, awkward, and unproductive—
even detrimental to the link between us as teacher and student. Where
Rose went on to graduate from community college, the others dropped
out of classes before the end of the term.

I had spent precious instructional minutes in classes taping our exchanges and then hours out of class transcribing tapes. Maybe my suggestions had not been helpful, but at least I had assumed that by observing
what happened between us, I would find out how we became derailed.
Disappointed and depressed, I asked myself, what did all these scraps of
paper tell me that was not common sense? What did they mean beyond
the obvious: Some students did well, and others less well? I suppose I
could say that Rose "showed" that these students had the ability to succeed and were not of such low IQ that (as Jensen said) they needed "training" and not "education."

In spite of their academic problems, Kelly and Mark came no closer
than Rose did to matching Jensen's portrait of the "Negro race" as mentally deficient and inevitably migrating to the least successful socioeco-
nomic class. Doubtless these young men's experiences and preferred
language were not those of school. As William Labov (1972c) concluded,
reading failure (and difficulties in other school areas as well) is "primarily

the result of political and cultural conflict within the classroom" (p. 35). As he also pointed out, pronunciation among young children and adolescents who spoke Black English differed from certain sounds of Standard English. Though the child may understand the meanings of *pass* and *past*, the two words sound the same to some Black youngsters. These differences could interfere with reading—especially in the primary grades—if teachers assumed the child must first be taught Standard English before tackling reading, writing, or math.

This misunderstanding on the part of the teacher was (and sometimes still is) a problem that has tangled many a low-tracked reading group. Labov and so many others have implied that such school problems stem from teachers' lack of will or knowledge to teach children in their classrooms. It was a refrain I had heard a million times, and once more the teacher came in for the blame. I knew, however, that structural and functional misunderstandings between teacher and student were more complicated than that analysis suggests.

So if the standard ways of explaining school failure were (to greater or lesser extent) flawed, what *did* explain failure? What learning environments led to success? What was I grasping for that stayed just out of reach? What were the questions that would satisfy me? If it had not been for Anthony, I might never have found a focus that would set me on the right track.

Because of what I learned from him, Anthony became that unforgettable student, the one who never goes completely out of mind. He entered college at age 27 or 28, or perhaps he was even older. He could have been 5'5" tall; he might have weighed 120 pounds. On the first day he wrote (or, more accurately, drew) a title and text that took up much of his single page: "I, Anthony Ward, want to be a football star." The O's in this opening statement were carefully drawn to look like miniature footballs complete with tiny stitching.

I, FINE ANTHONY WARD WANT TO BE A FOOTBALL STAR

> That is what I want to be so that is why I'm at laney because I want
> to be recognized as a Hollwood star. People say that I'm to little to
> play football. But they do not know what I can do with a football. You
> know they don't know what I'd going to do out their on the field.

Print removes from the text exactly the features that touched me most. Each letter was hand drawn. In spite of various incompatibilities—his small size and his unrealistic notions about stars, football, and Hollywood—I still recognized determination. Anthony had a wish to do something with his life. I could work with that.

Anthony had style, too, both in his dress and as a leader to those who surrounded him. Women and men sat outside our classroom in the bleacher seats that surrounded the college's swimming pool, waiting for him to finish class. Even as the fall semester brought West Coast rain, he dressed in a long coat of fine wool with a velveteen collar, nipped in at the waist and flaring past the knees. Elegant from the neat, small-brimmed hat he wore to his well-shined boots: This is the snapshot I have kept with me, for that is the way he looked on the day I found the focus that would guide my work for many years. I was still a long way from a precise question, but I never again wondered if I had anything worth thinking about.

And yet it was largely luck that brought me to this critical moment of teaching and learning. Since I had given up on audiotape and turned to video because most audiotapes were useless, full of the sounds of scraping chairs or students writing quietly, it just happened that I could not only hear but see a complete text of the exchange between Anthony and me. Portable video technology had not been available long, and the BETA format was clunky and awkward. Yet I felt lucky to be part of that first wave of researchers who could rely on a machine's accurate representation. Without both seeing and hearing what went on—and being able to relive and reflect upon these awkward and embarrassing moments over innumerable playbacks—our exchanges would have become vague and would finally have evaporated like ephemeral conversation.

When I first reviewed the videotape, I was tempted to erase those of my comments in which I was less than sensitive. But in the interest of seeing it as it was and not as I thought was proper, the whole exchange stood before me—the good, the awkward, and the puzzling. The conversation took place in the same classroom where I had worked with Mark and Kelly. Anthony had placed himself in the back of the room, as he always did, and plenty of empty desks surrounded us since the semester was half over. Other tutors were doing roughly the same thing I was: helping students get ideas on paper or listening to them read papers aloud. As I reached Anthony's desk, I saw only a blank sheet titled "A So-Called Friend." Realizing he had been staring at it for a while, I approached him with a pocketful of teaching experience. Determined to get him started writing fluently instead of sweating over each word, I asked him to tell me more about this friend. For about 20 minutes—a long, slow 20 minutes—we went from his single-syllable replies to his story of a friend's betrayal. But it was not until later that I understood what had happened in that conversation and what effect it had on learning.

So, what did I learn from these transcripts? The first section shows I did most of the talking. He answered as briefly as possible, and we had several minor misunderstandings:

SMOKEY: OK, so it's really *not* about a so-called friend?
ANTHONY: Yeah.
SMOKEY: What are you gonna tell about?
ANTHONY: I don't know yet. Jes' about thangs [things] that happen in the past.
SMOKEY: Mmmm . . .
ANTHONY: Oh, what I'm saying about now?
SMOKEY: *Yeah.* About this guy [reading from the page]: "I met a friend in the 6th grade and . . ." He's the so-called friend, right? And a so-called friend to *me* means he's not really not a very good friend.
ANTHONY: Right.
SMOKEY: Is that—are you gonna make that point?
ANTHONY: Yeah.

We were stumbling. His answers—"Yeah" or "Right"—were answers that did not match my questions. The next exchange became progressively worse, with misunderstandings at all levels. Sometimes perfectly ordinary words drew responses I did not expect, such as his response "Jes' thangs that happen in the past," when I expected him to give details of a specific event. At other times, I failed to understand even words I knew. I had to stop and think that "fo hunnert" was "four hundred." The most damaging misunderstanding was my failure to understand the one word on which the point of his story depended: "crep,'" (or "crept" in Standard English). Only through his repeated gestures did I finally understand: His friend "stole" his money. When I finally understood him, a qualitative change in his talk appeared:

SMOKEY: Well, what did he do?
ANTHONY: Took a li'l money from me.
SMOKEY: How much [laugh] two dollars?
ANTHONY: fo hunnert.
SMOKEY: Oh that's good. Is—was—is that the occasion for the, uh, fight between you?
ANTHONY: Naw, they ain't no fight. Just, uh, you'd be surprised what people do these days, you can't trust nobody that's all. I wouldn'a expected him to treat me like that, thass [that's] all.
SMOKEY: OK, this is a man you knew from 6th grade who you thought you have every reason to trust.
ANTHONY: Yeah, thought he wouldn't sting me like that.
SMOKEY: And instead . . . as soon as you gave him the money . . . What? Can you tell the situation?
ANTHONY: I didn't G-I-I-IVE him no money. He crep' on my pocket like my coat was layin down in my house n' [he gestures, reaching hand into inside jacket pocket]. You know where I keep mine, you know, getting ready for school.

SMOKEY: And you had your money in your pocket, and . . .

ANTHONY: So I laid my coat down wash my face, you know, run through the hall. He crep' on me, see . . . [He gestures, hand inside pocket]. He crep on me see and slob . . . and I wouln'ta expected it.

SMOKEY: [laughs] That's good. So now that explains why he's a so-called friend, that's *good*. Do you think . . .

ANTHONY: I wouldn't care if he stole ten or twenty dollars or something but fo' hunert dollars, thass *too* much to say "forget about it," you know, just throw it away, shit.

The final section of this conversation ended with Anthony doing all the talking—what those who study conversation call "holding the floor"—his story pouring out. We had come a long way from "Jes' thangs that happen in the past." After our conversation, Anthony sat down and wrote his story:

So one day my so call friend came over my house before I went to school. So you know I thought maybe he came over that moning to smoke some weed or something with me, But you know what he did. He went into my pocket and took . . . Four hundred dollars of my money. You can mist around with women but not my money. You know I had my money in my inside pocket. I went into the Bathroom to wash my face. So when I did that he went into my pocket. My coat was on the couch. So Right to day I do not have me a so call friend.

My use-to-be so-called friend is doing six more months in jail wright to day. That what he gets for stealing from me.

Fine Anthony Ward
Wa$
Hi$
Be$t
Friend

With the newly written version of "A So-Called Friend, Part 2" and the videotape in my briefcase, I was all but skipping down the concrete steps that led to the parking lot. I went straight home and started the video. As I listened to the tape over and over, I realized how little I had understood of what he had said during those minutes in the classroom. Only after many hours did I notice and appreciate his colorful and subtle oral style. The differently stressed word, the place of gesture, variations in rhythms and tone of voice—these so-called paralinguistic or nonverbal features carried information I had expected to be put into words.

The tape showed me I had not been the scintillating teacher of my fantasies. Still, the samples of spoken and written language were valuable. I had seen learning in situ. I had seen how the dialog between us had led to a change in his writing, from a few thrown-together sentences to the beginning of a personal-experience narration. I had not seen this change in Mark's or Kelly's writing. If Rose had had similar exchanges, I had neither witnessed nor participated in them. I had witnessed Anthony's writing change in a single sitting—from the vague "Jes' about thangs that happen in the past" to a specific event that became the bones of a narrative, bones he could build on. I had seen learning.

Back to the library that week, I was on fire with the glimmer of an alternative to the usual two choices—school failure as either the fault of child or the fault of institution. Maybe the problems could be recast somehow, not as broad abstractions but as specific, observable classroom events. Through our stumbling, I found the focus that drove much of my future work.

IN THEORY: MICROANALYSIS APPEARS

The broad theories about thought and language that became basic readings in the courses I took were not all that new when I first learned about them. Gregory Bateson had written essays in the 1950s that I read much later in a collection entitled *Steps to an Ecology of Mind* (2000). John Dewey and Lev Vygotsky were publishing during the 1930s although Vygotsky's work was not widely available in English until the 1970s.

These thinkers had been largely ignored in American schools of education during the period when behaviorism dominated, when only that which could be seen and counted was regarded as scientific. But slowly, over the next decades, this view began to change.

New Assumptions About Cognitive Development

Bateson spoke about "mind" and consciousness, Vygotsky about "higher orders" of thought, Dewey about educating the whole child rather than training for a particular response through reinforcement. More and more, qualitative and ethnographic approaches were recognized and began to take their place alongside quantitative measures. Theories about cognition and language use in daily life became central.

Bateson (2000) opened his collection of essays and lectures by outlining a "new way of thinking about *ideas* and about those aggregates of ideas which I call *minds*" (p. xxiii). Of the many contributions Bateson made to my grasp of the concept of "mind," perhaps the most important was his theory that we acquire our ideas in contexts or settings that promote learning. We *learn* to learn. But what if the classroom is not a context in which one learns to learn? Could that be a piece of the puzzle I needed in order to understand what had happened to Rose and Mark and so many others?

The psychologist Lev Vygotsky also offered me rich ways to envision the mind at work maturing. Like Bateson, he sought to unify psychology so that both stimulus-response and big-picture thinking could serve as lenses to seek out new meanings, and he sought the relation between thought and language, mind and society. I pored over two volumes that had been translated in 1962 and 1978 and found immediate application to my questions in his notion of the "zone of proximal development." *Proximal* means "near," and we could understand this "near space" as a point for incipient growth.

As Vygotsky describes the learning situation, a child's "spontaneous concepts" are those drenched in the youngster's experience. The formalized knowledge of science is the adults' domain and operates by abstraction. Little by little, the child's "bottom-up" learning and abstraction's "top-down" teaching meet and become mutually explanatory. Something similar, I realized, was happening in the interaction between Anthony and me. He "knew" his experience; I knew some things about writing that made his experience visible.

In order to observe this process of cognitive maturation, Vygotsky argued, we would gain a more sensitive measure of learners' thinking if we study not only what the child can already do independently, but the upcoming stage of growth—the actions the youngsters can perform with coaching from a more expert aide. This point of development is that moment when "a child's rich experience and disorganized concepts would meet the systematic structure and logic of adult reasoning" (Vygotsky, 1978, pp. xxvii–xxix). Vygotsky (1978) described processes of an unfolding mental maturity as taking place in the zone of proximal development:

> We propose that an essential feature of learning is that it creates the zone of proximal development; that is, learning awakens a variety of internal developmental processes that are able to operate only when the child is interacting with people in his environment and in cooperation with his peers. Once the processes are internalized, they become part of the child's independent developmental achievement. The zone of proximal development defines those functions that have not yet matured but are in the process of maturation. . . . These functions could be termed the "buds" . . . rather than the "fruits" of development. (pp. 86, 90)

I was excited by Bateson's and Vygotsky's emphasis on the importance of ideas placed in meaningful contexts, and on how learning often depends on symbiotic relations between the learner and the more expert or experienced peer.

Vygotsky's theories about thinking and learning as taking place in relation with others are now widely assumed have even become all but clichés. Nevertheless, since the common belief in the 1960s and 1970s was that reading and writing were solitary activities, Bateson's and Vygotsky's ideas began to clarify vague notions of language and thought processes.

New Assumptions About Language

The study of language, like the study of cognition and learning, had undergone its own evolution due to much the same notions that motivated the new understanding of "mind." In fact, at that point in my research, I could no longer envision hard and fast distinctions between thought, language, and culture. By the late 1970s, no one in graduate school could read widely without encountering references to new understandings of language: Be it verbal, nonverbal, or a shared mental schema, how do two people recognize one another's meanings?

Gregory Bateson (2000) interpreted these nonverbal signals as meta-communication. One day in the San Francisco zoo, he saw "two young monkeys *playing,* i.e., engaged in an interactive sequence of which the . . . signals were similar to but not the same as those of combat" (p. 177). How did they *know* not to draw blood? Researchers in multiple disciplines began to examine such nonverbal means of communication. Was it possible to communicate nothing while one stands at a bus stop? The sociologist Erving Goffman (1963) showed that the organization of gatherings, of behavior in public places, makes it impossible to avoid communicating something, even through silence. *Involvement* with our fellows is inevitable, even when "walking down the street" (pp. 8–9).

How had the field moved from the study of abstract structures to the study of everyday talk? This major shift in linguistics did not happen overnight. From it I learned perhaps my first important lesson about scholarship: It builds on previous work, and builds and builds, until other scholars begin to ask questions about problems the major theory does not address. And then there are more and more questions that generate new studies, until finally the weight of the new work begins to undermine the old, nudges it, so to speak, into new directions.

In this case, what was "undermined"—or at least what shifted—was Noam Chomsky's idea of "a consideration of the structure of the sentence"(1967, p. 169), as he had explained it in his review of B. F. Skinner's analysis of verbal behavior. Central to Chomsky's ideas, as I understood his work, was that language existed in abstract "deep structures" in speakers' minds. When prodded, so to speak, by the speaker's wish to say something, a series of mental "transformations" operated on the deep structures to give a spoken "surface structure." The tricky part, of course, was inferring these transformations from what speakers say inasmuch as they took place in the mind and without conscious awareness. The goal was to explain how all sentences are formed. Careful examining of syntactic structures raised more and more questions about word meanings and about semantics—questions once thought to be answerable by syntax rules alone.

John Austin (1962) was one of the landmark theorists who argued that, no matter how straightforward some sentences seemed, they had no efficacy unless spoken by the right person at the right time. "I thee wed" or "I censure you" were more—much more—than subject-verb-object statements; they were in fact a special kind of sentence that showed language as an *act* that is embedded in social context and having a particular force.

John Searle's (1975) work on indirect speech acts added to this notion of language as an act. He demonstrated how often a sentence states one thing but means something else. Searle's oft-quoted example–"Can you pass the salt?" (a question that does not inquire about a broken arm but indirectly asks for the salt)—illustrates the difference between what a sentence *says* and what a speaker *means* (p. 61).

I felt at once that this contribution to the exploration of daily talk could have implications for some students' problems in school.

But scholarship progresses slowly. Paul Grice (1975) made another step beyond the word and the sentence by taking an interest in conversation as a whole, in discourse. He imagined conversations and proposed that, to assure cooperation in conversation, comments must be clear, brief, and direct (pp. 43–45). Almost at once, other linguists pointed out that real language was not what Grice imagined. Indeed, people do not always convey direct messages when they speak, such as "Close that window!" Instead, they may want to assure at the same time that neither speaker nor addressee loses face, with statements such as "It's freezing here! That open window . . ."

Robin Lakoff (1979) said that speakers are often not direct at all, but indirect. Lakoff's principles for conversational cooperation conflicted with Grice's ideas. In one of her lectures, she said that when maintaining a relationship is important, we try not to impose on others' wishes or personal space; we offer alternatives to give the other person options. Above all, she emphasizes, speakers spend considerable energy protecting rapport or camaraderie: With social equals we ask, not demand.

As theory shifted from abstract structures to everyday talk, from syntax (or grammar) to pragmatics (socially appropriate speech), research became especially useful to studies of schooling. When two friends lose camaraderie on the playground, they can quickly patch it up. When a teacher fails to maintain rapport with her 25 or more charges, the classroom atmosphere sours. Disgruntled students, offended over and over, often become resistant toward the teacher and toward the information the curriculum provides. Teachers, resisted over and over, often become discouraged and hardened. From a sociologist's viewpoint, these cracks in relationships echo power constructs in social roles and norms almost below our active level of awareness.

Penelope Brown and Stephen Levinson (1987) also authored an important work in pragmatics in which they identify *politeness phenomena* as features that provide a special link between language and society. A speaker's way of talking—their body language and tone of voice—can make the addressee either lose face (*negative face*) or keep face (*positive face*). When an addressee feels threatened, the speaker can remove the threat and help the addressee save face. In daily affairs, if and when face is called into question, speakers must do so in carefully conventionalized ways. Issues involved in maintaining or losing face include the relative power of speaker over addressee, the social distance between the two, and the degree of imposition in the request or demand the speaker makes. As Brown and Levinson see it, these ideas are deeply bound up with self-esteem and personhood, and of course with many school interactions (pp. 13, 61–73).

These new territories—semantics and pragmatics, speech acts and words beyond the sentence, or discourse—changed linguistics, which had once been bounded by phonology, lexicon, and syntax. Language in use began to seem very different from sentences in a grammar book. I turned all these new tools toward my classroom: conversational competence; paralinguistic signals, including the almost invisible *hedge* ("I kinda think"); back-channel cues ("uh-huh," nods, and "Really?" inserted into conversations in just the right rhythm); and other such features as described by Yngve in 1970 and Schegloff in 1982. I did not know it at the beginning, but all these terms would soon be fleshed out as I sought to discover what worked and what went wrong.

How better to understand Anthony's initial resistance to talking with the teacher than by reference to his being caught off guard or threatened with loss of face? How often had Anthony been asked to speak and, at the same time, sensed criticism for speaking in the dialect he knew best or for using words teachers judged inappropriate? Had he been forced into verbal corners in front of the class before he shrank away from giving any answer at all? Whatever had made Anthony so guarded, just like Rose's refusal to read aloud in 10th grade, suggested ways failure might begin. Reading some of Gregory Bateson's articles, such as "Culture Contact and Schismogenesis" (1935) and "A Theory of Play and Fantasy" (1955), recently collected in his book *Steps to an Ecology of Mind* (2000), I began to understand the risks and the possibilities of cross-cultural contact and about the damaging effects on speakers who get in trouble when they do or do not respond.

A window opened. I could see the classroom as a place where certain learners risk loss of face on a daily basis. In a dialog, when one person holds power over others and ranks higher in social status, she also holds the right to impose her demands on others. In the classroom, that is practically a job description for teachers: They hold the power of punishment or reward, they have the "right" of higher social status, and, moreover, they impose requests and demands upon their pupils. "Who can sit with hands folded until the bell?" "Sam, what are you doing?" These orders, concealed as questions, seem to say one thing but actually say another entirely. They can make students who do not share instructors' conversational assumptions particularly vulnerable.

But teachers also fear vulnerability: That is at least one reason it is hard to admit to a lack of knowledge or a moment of uncertainty. In a multicultural classroom, possible threats to face and self-esteem increase dramatically for both student and teacher.

Studies of Classroom Interaction

The new work on classroom interaction helped explain what might go wrong and began to suggest some remedies. To build a framework, I followed various studies about interactions as they constructed classroom life and affected students' learning of school skills (Gumperz, 1982a; Philips, 1972; Jupp, Roberts, & Cook-Gumperz, 1978; Scollon & Scollon, 1981; see also Erickson 1982). Many of these studies found that classroom talk affected learning and literacy. It was a relatively new idea that ordinary talk—something as ephemeral as conversation—could affect a life's trajectory. Yet when a reading group placement or promotion is based primarily on language, these ephemera result in inflexible decisions about a student's readiness progress (see Mehan, 1974).

Several studies, for example, showed how particular rhetorical styles made a difference in how children were treated in classrooms. Collins and Michaels (1986) described how much more schoolwork was accomplished in "high" reading groups than in the disjointed and chaotic "low" reading groups. In a now-famous 1st-grade "sharing time" study, Michaels (1986) told of a 1st-grade teacher engaged in sharing where one child is allowed to stand up and hold the floor until she has told the rest of the class about her news or a favorite toy. This teacher favored children whose sharing contribution was "explicit and [whose] narrative is tightly structured upon a single event" (p. 102). Moreover, children who did not exhibit this style were interrupted during their share ("share" is the name given to these speeches). In an informal interview 18 months after the 1st-grade study, one girl told the researcher: "Sharing time got on my nerves. She was always interruptin' me, sayin' 'that's not important enough'" (p. 110).

Students who used less preferred speaking styles in school settings were repeatedly asked to sit down. One of the less preferred styles, for example, came to be called a "high-involvement" style. This is a style that chains together several topics and relies less on words and full sentences than on shared background knowledge, miming or acting out certain parts of a story, and waiting for others' "Uh-huh" or "Really." Anthony's narrative shows a use of this style. He began in the "defensive monosyllabic style" that Labov had noticed in testing situations, sounding as if he had "no language," but he helped the teacher understand via a high-involvement style and finally settled into narration.

When listeners are not picking up certain verbal signals, when teachers inaccurately interpret what the learner is trying to say, communication fails. These failures can have dire results. We all know—and studies describe—the difficulties for the minority student at all levels of education as well as in the workplace. Communication problems arise when speakers do not share the rhetorical styles preferred—and expected—by the person in power. But once we become aware of these problems as they arise, mistakes can be repaired. It is tricky, but it is what this book is about.

In Response: A Focus at Last

When I started graduate school, I learned to rein in my personal reactions to research that labeled students like those I taught as genetically and socially disadvantaged and scarcely fit for school. I learned how to offer refutations in the reasoned and "objective" tone preferred in academic circles. But reading ethnomethodologists like Hugh Mehan (1974) and conversational analysts like John Gumperz (1982a) was one of the most satisfying moments I had in graduate school. In them I saw the work of the 1960s summarily dismissed, and I was equally pleased to note the role language played in the work of these researchers.

There were those—in fact, a great many of those—who had rejected the deficit models. But I was reminded of those old reactions I had tamped down while thinking about the deficit model: I was disturbed by the underlying negative and accusatory attitudes toward classroom teachers that the articles sometimes implied. I could not help wondering if the researchers had ever had to manage 30 wiggly 1st graders. Classroom observers taped daily activities, collected children's work, and helped out in some teachers' classrooms. These assistants were grateful for the time and for what they had learned about schooling, yet often they also cast a negative light on what they had observed.

Over time, the suggestions of condescension added up. No special study, no one author is to blame, but I suppose I had finally had enough of the undercurrent of teacher bashing—implicit if not outspoken—that appeared so often in university research. I vowed to take on classroom research from teachers' perspectives in studies that treated evenhandedly the problematic clashes between teacher and student. I would accomplish it, I decided, through studying interactions and applying the research methods that I thought held promise for showing us our classrooms.

As I began to distinguish between implicit criticisms and the techniques conversational analysis made possible, I simmered down. And thereby hangs the problem with judgments made by outsiders: While only a teacher can evaluate what is going on in a moment of classroom time, this same teacher must monitor her own behavior and language at that same moment, and she must be ruthlessly honest about what she sees about her instruction.

I could be my own case in point. I had assumed no outside visitor would ever hear misunderstandings between me and my students. In fact, I would have thought I never had such misunderstandings. However, as I listened over and over to that videotaped exchange with Anthony, I recognized my own difficulties—and they were not too different from those that Michaels and others had observed in their studies. At the beginning, my conversation with Anthony had been tough sledding. Listening to the tape I could hear how often I had failed to understand him. He had had to work very hard, but his patient use of repeated mime (placing his hand in an imaginary coat pocket) and his emphatic speech led to my breakthrough in recognizing "crep'" as "stole."

With a class of 30 students waiting for my instruction, I could not have taken the 20 minutes I used with Anthony from class time. In the regular classroom, I most likely would never have gotten to the narrative's point, the very point that made his friend a "so-called friend." And, of course, teachers do not usually have the luxury of extended writing conferences. But in these one-to-one settings, I sought strategies that could help me and other teachers like me work together with their students toward full academic literacy. There was a mountain of work remaining before reaching that goal, and the answers often seemed desperately far away.

Part III

COLLECTING ARTIFACTS

The chapters in Part III—"Darleen: Reading Beyond Skills" and "Gloria and Ruth: Student–Teacher Interactions"—concentrate on the conversations between teachers or tutors and their students. The first, a case study of a teacher and a single learner and her tape-recorded reading journals, shows smooth communications between teacher and student. The second, a comparison of two students as they interact with tutors about their essays, shows how the quality of student–teacher communication can vary.

These glimpses into interactions between teachers and students—via transcriptions of recorded conversations and pieces of writing—illustrate two kinds of data and evidence that can be studied.

The teacher-researcher can focus her lens on many different kinds of classroom products and processes to better understand her question. A partial list is provided in the "Guide." The choice, of course, should fit the question; its analysis should either affirm or negate the main question of the study.

Chapter 5

—

Darleen:
Literacy Beyond Skills

How can I guide reading in a whole-class setting using the techniques I learned to guide writing?

While my work in the Writing Center was going on along one track, new semesters and new students inevitably appeared. I had been assigned a basic reading class, and I was itching to relate what I was testing in the composition class to teaching reading. The problem, of course, was that reading is silent and invisible. Students can be engaged in discussing their writing with a prompt like "Tell me more," but we do not often talk in the same way about reading, an act in which they have to follow another's ideas and events. How could I use what I knew about student–teacher interaction with readers in a classroom setting?

I was determined to learn to guide reading in the same way that I was learning to guide writing. Remembering Mark and Kelly, I asked myself, "Do you dare rely upon a curriculum in reading that has interaction as its base?" I reduced my case of nerves by turning, in my mind, from my role as front-line teacher to that of classroom researcher. By viewing this class as an extension of the questions I had been probing, I calmed my teaching anxiety.

In Practice

My reading class that year, sometime in the early 1980s, was greatly over-subscribed; I lost count at 30 students. One of the faces in the crunch—one of those I told to come back next semester and "Register early!"—was Darleen. I sounded less than cordial to my own ears, but she waited until after class and asked again if she could join. I do not remember exactly what I said, but I think I said, "not this term." Unknown to me, however, one of our old hands, a tutor who had been around almost as long as I had, pulled her aside and told her that if she would wait a few days until everything settled down, we would probably find her a place. And so it was.

I went into class knowing what I wanted to try but not knowing what form it would take. I knew I needed to document what happened. Somehow I had to watch students reading, but since reading was internal, pulling that off would be a real trick.

All that I had studied stood me in good stead. I held on mightily to Vygotsky's description of learning—that zone of proximal development, that "near next step" in the development of higher cognitive functioning that a learner cannot yet make independently but can achieve with the guidance of a more experienced guide. My practice so far—my work with Anthony and the tutors' work with their students—had confirmed his ideas in action. It was upon me now to discover the next step. Could I use with a large reading class what had worked effectively one-on-one in composition? In the end, all my stewing about what I had undertaken was resolved serendipitously and unexpectedly by a part of my reading curriculum.

Darleen was an unprepossessing beginner. She was quiet, very quiet. Not for months did I come to know anything about her, and what I learned was mostly indirect. She was in her late 30s. She had her first child when she was 18 or 19, and she and her husband reared three children. She wrote once that she was "pure Puerto Rican," but her father had been born in Hawai'i and her mother within a few blocks of the same street where Darleen and her youngsters all grew up. The limitations she faced in reading and writing were my concern. She was, she said, out of practice, very much so. She tested well below 6th-grade level.

I was not a novice at teaching reading. I had taught when the reading program had only a few magazines for materials. I had taught under government grants, in which skills were carefully divided into pronunciation, vocabulary, and comprehension, and where comprehension was further divided into factual and interpretive processes. I had taught about vocabulary in context. I had taught roots and prefixes and suffixes. I had taught multiple word meanings and comprehension. I had used those endless workbook exercises entitled "Get the Facts!" and "Find the Main Idea!"

Ultimately, though, a past teaching experience had turned me away from conventional skill-based instruction—it was the day my Old Reliable lesson on chronological narrative sequence failed. As I wrote *sequence* on the board, I asked the conventional opener: "Who knows what *sequence* means?"

A student's hand shot up, one of my favorite students, to report that she knew: "sequence" were those, "um, shiny things I had on my prom dress." I had wanted students to relate "sequencing" to the comprehension framework I had been working on in the "Elements of Reading," but she confirmed what I had suspected: I had built that framework in a vacuum, unrelated to students or their experiences, or to what they needed.

It was a watershed moment of embarrassment for me. Yes, I had been around the basic-reading-course block a time or two, but after this my standby lessons became less trustworthy. They had done nothing that showed me students discovering that bookish intimacy I had had with all those books I had grown up with—the Sue Barton nurse series and the Nancy Drew mystery series—nothing to help them catch my passion for reading. I had been teaching skills I hoped they would need later—material they did not use, did not even know they needed. So they went on saying, "Reading is boring."

Eventually I came to understand how to use skill-and-drill materials, but the whole instructional problem was one, interestingly enough, of sequencing. When was the right time to introduce skills? I had always taught them first, before real reading, before students learned to care about books. It was not until this class that I stripped away the worksheets and returned to the students, the texts, and the teacher.

It was risky, for the pressure to teach this skill or that one is always strong. For this course, I prepared a "reader" comprised of short two- to three-page essays and stories, including favorites by writers like Gordon Parks (who became a famous photographer and Renaissance Man, but only after spending 20 years in the school of hard knocks), my own writing, and students' writings from previous years. I thought that the collection was a winner, that students should be able to find one or more pieces of writing that they could connect with. Even so, I still had stage fright that first day because I knew we were going to try to read in a new way, but I did not know exactly what that would be.

My first brave new assignment was a bust. I asked students to begin a "tell me about what you read" reading journal, in which they would write about what they had read, and to which I would respond. No one did; not one notebook came in. But I had learned to choose my battles. If an assignment was boycotted by the whole class, I had better let it fade away. Something else, something new: How could I find the bookish intimacy I sought?

I replaced that first assignment with one I had figured out when I could not sleep: a tape-recorded reading journal. Here, finally, I hit on something that satisfied both my students and me. Students brought in an audiotape (or used one I supplied), selected one or two paragraphs from a reading they had liked that week, and read their selections onto audiotape. Then they added a comment about why they had chosen this particular passage, *why*, as I said over and over, it had been meaningful. I listened and then recorded my responses, saying something about the "critical reading" the students had done, the moment in which students apparently had captured some important theme in their lives. Then I might have added a comment about how smoothly they had read (their "fluency") and the word or words that they needed help pronouncing or understanding.

At first I planned to use the tape recordings to look for breakdowns in communication between students and me, miscommunications that prevented learning but that could perhaps be repaired. But then came a serendipitous moment: One student—so flat in affect, so self-protective—startled me by showing not blocks to learning, but the kind of transformation I knew reading could, and should, offer. It was through these taped dialogs that Darleen wound her way into and around much of what I had been thinking about.

Her first reading had struck me as being of no moment. She had read the previous day's class assignment into the recorder, and I responded by telling her she could read anything she wanted from the class reader, but, sensing her tension from the ragged breathiness of her voice, I suggested she relax.

Her second recording showed a stronger voice, a more confident one. Although she had not yet grasped "selecting one important part," she read a two-page essay written by another student about learning to drive. I had anticipated her comment to describe her own driving experience, but her interpretation went in a different direction altogether:

> I don't drive. Lotta times I have the nerve to get up and do it but then I back away. Like everything else, you have to take that first step and maybe someday I'll end up taking that step to drive too. Like everything else, I'm nervous to drive. I don't find myself doing that.

I looked across the great chasm between my life and hers—I had never even thought about being afraid of driving like that, but I had other anxieties and fears. I understood the impact of that fear. I imagined the countless bus stops where she and her children had waited. I put the first reading and the second one together and responded:

> Learning how to drive is no joke. You might want to try some things that help you get over your nervousness. I'm really impressed that you are trying so hard to improve your reading when I know it makes you nervous.

A few weeks later, she selected a new text for her assignment, a handout I had written about the development of the English language, "History of English." In her interpretation of it, she added to her developing theme of questioning herself as a reader:

I'm finding out more and more each day that I read that I understand English more, and the more I read the more I like it. There's a lot more for me to learn, but it's a start and I think I'm headed in the right direction. And that's why I picked this story. The story "History of English" is very fascinating to read.

Knowledge is power. Somehow, knowing about the language was "fascinating" because she was engaged with gaining information, with reading, and with her own learning. For me, as well, there was a new kind of knowledge: How to use what I had learned in writing conferences in a new context.

In fact, Darleen's work helped me realize that linking "school problems" with "miscommunication," as I had been thinking, was too narrow an answer. Maybe the difficulties had other sources and other remedies as well. Important to me at the moment, however, was that I had begun to see how to move away from one-on-one talk to working with an entire class while still retaining guidance toward making the next development step, the "next step" of Vygotsky's "zone of proximal development." And I had begun to see how technology could work to students' benefit: Tape-recording had enabled proximal development to move from face-to-face contact to long-distance communication. In fact, I wondered if the tape-recording had helped free Darleen from the immediacy of face-to-face contact and actually made learning easier. In the course of the semester, she learned a lot using those tapes, including how to give a summary and how to discuss plot and character. As the semester ended, she concluded one entry by saying "Well, Smokey, thanks for letting me read this book. I really enjoyed it. . . ."

After that semester, she continued in basic classes and later moved on to credit-bearing courses until, at last, she received her 2-year degree in child development.

And how did I assess my own progress? Since interactions of certain kinds helped some students with writing, I had wanted to understand if interactions were also helpful with reading. If I had to speak with a school board or my dean, how I could justify that "real reading" should come first and skill instruction later, sometimes much later? For a better grasp of these aspects of my questions, I turned again to the educational psychology library to find what had been written about reading and literacy.

In Theory: Social Construction Emerges

The study of reading has always been tangled. The mix contains teachers' conventional wisdom of how to teach as well as researchers' slow progress at understanding the nature of reading. In spite of the shared subject, however, their different approaches often set them at loggerheads (Chall, 1996). Then, too, teachers and researchers have long had their battles. As teachers perceive it, those who spend their life "studying reading" offer them too few practical ideas. But researchers also have complaints: Classrooms are "hidebound" and school sites refuse researchers' experiments to find better ways. Accordingly, the split continually widens. Just as researchers rarely listen to teachers, teachers often do not listen to news from academia.

I have felt the frustrations from both sides. As I dug into the research on reading, questions multiplied—and answers divided. After all, direction from the academic world changes frequently. But while some teachers react contemptuously to this constant re-visioning, I found the newer visions increasingly interesting. The new theories, new experiments, new methods, and new findings offered more productive ways of asking questions about reading. Is reading a social act? Or is it instead a deeply private one? What is the nature of reading and how can it best be taught? Among these tangles and uncertainties, I needed to sort out how I was going to answer these questions for my own work.

A central problem in the study of reading has been one of vocabulary. For example, teachers speak of *decoding* or *phonics*, teaching methods that point out regularities in the English spelling system. Researchers speak of *phonemes* and *graphemes*, or of the *alphabetic principle*, terms that do not refer, exactly, to the "sounds" of the language, but rather to possible—that is, meaningful—contrastive sounds: *p* versus *b*, *f* versus *v*, and so on. Similar word jumbles plague discussions of other aspects of reading such as *critical reading, critical thinking,* and *literary criticism.* Do they share meanings?

Skill-Based Reading Instruction

Classroom instruction about reading is often based on conventional wisdom: Teachers learn what to do by watching other reading teachers. One reading expert, Jeanne Chall, examined teaching and research from 1910 to 1965, looking especially at the sight-word method ("see and say") and the phonics approach ("sounding out") in *Learning to Read: The Great Debate* (1967). In that volume, as well as in articles published 30 years later, she championed the phonics approach as part of the "pedagogical mainstream effectively employed for more than fifty years" (1996, p. 310).

Emphasis on Decoding Skills. Paul Rozin and Lila R. Gleitman (1977) studied beginning reading, and put into words one aspect of what makes reading acquisition so difficult: "The alphabet is based on a segmentation of the sound stream in terms of . . . units . . . represented only indirectly in the acoustic wave" (p. 58). After a survey of massive quantities of published findings, the authors conclude that "phonological awareness" is critical in early stages of reading.

These authors feel, however, that it is not the letter-by-letter sound-symbol awareness that matters, but rather the sound-symbol correspondence at the level of the syllable. For the nonsense sequence "ROBATILIF-IC" Rosen and Gleitman (1977) say that readers most likely do not identify sounds letter by letter—Ruh-O-Buh-A, and so on—but rather "work syllable by syllable, roughly RO-BA-TA-LI-FIC" (pp. 84–85). The syllable, then, is most likely a necessary middle ground between "learning to read" and "reading fluently" (p. 71).

When Rozin and Gleitman's study first appeared, researchers hailed it as definitive. They admired the synthesis of experimental findings and the clearly stated conclusions drawn from the data. In contrast, when teachers read or heard about the findings, many commented, "So? What's new?" or "We've known that forever." Reading teachers did not understand the fuss over old news, even though in fact they did not recognize what was new about Rozin and Gleitman's findings. In the end, the researchers felt their contribution was ill-received.

Emphasis on Comprehension Skills. Reading research had been important even before Chall's publication in 1967. If we regard reading the way we would an archeological site, we see theories in layers from various time periods, and ironically, the views of reading that researchers have turned away from are exactly the views schools put into practice now.

During and after World War II millions of Americans took reading tests, and statistics allowed national scores to be analyzed and interpreted. By 1944, the search for the mechanics of reading had begun in earnest. Frederick B. Davis's (1944) early skill-based theory identified a set of reading skills, from which Davis isolated two as essential: knowledge of word meanings and ability to draw inferences. Along with others judged as being less essential, these are still found on reading skill lists today: grasp of facts, recognition of writer's purpose, attitude, tone and mood, identification of a writer's techniques such as literary devices, and passage structure.

Models of Reading: Mechanical Acts

Researchers interested in information processing studied reading as a useful model for artificial intelligence, or AI. One widely known model, Phillip Gough's "One Second of Reading" (in Singer & Ruddell, 1976),

was studied carefully by teacher-trainers and others interested in computer technology. In that model, Gough developed a flowchart that tracked
the lightning speed of comprehension: moving instantly from sentence
input to reader understanding, from eye to ear to brain, to TPWSGWTAU
(The Place Where Sentences Go When They Are Understood).

Models of Reading: Psycholinguistic Acts

In that same decade a third wave of researchers who were interested
in psycholinguistics also designed reading models as flowcharts. While
Gough concentrated on the route from input to output, the charts shaped
by the psycholinguistic researchers added "human" factors (Ruddell,
1974). Robert Ruddell's chart included memory, semantic and syntactic
information, readers' experiences, cognitive strategies, and emotional mo-
bilizers (Singer & Ruddell, 1976, p. 465).

Other psycholinguists showed a special interest in teaching children
as well as in theory-making. They hypothesized that readers' command of
oral language was the primary way of making sense out of printed matter. Kenneth and Yetta Goodman (1967) describe reading as a "psycholinguistic guessing game" in which readers use multiple cues from both oral
and written language to understand what they read. Based on this idea of
the meaningfulness of print, their diagnostic test, the Miscue Reading In-
ventory, provided teachers with a set of full-length stories, which learners
read aloud while teachers noted poorly placed pauses or deviations from
the printed text on a separate copy. Deviations that indicated poor use of
context clues or word calling were treated as serious errors; mistakes that
substituted a word that was correct in meaning though wrong in letter
pattern were treated as less serious errors.

All these notions of reading shared one important basic assumption:
that reading is communication—that is, a piece of reading has a message,
a single discoverable meaning. This assumption, for generations taken for
granted, would come into question during the waves of research in the
1980s and thereafter. During the same years that Ruddell's System of Communication appeared in textbooks for preservice secondary and elementary teachers, other researchers in rhetoric, literary criticism, sociolinguistics,
and composition began moving the entire discussion about reading into
new territory. Under the various banners of postmodernism, feminism,
deconstruction, and social construction, these disciplines offered infinitely
broader definitions of reading and identified new functions. Except for the
work of the Goodmans, the first three waves of research offered little that
clarified what I was working out with Darleen.

A Major Shift: From Reading to Literacy

I had already surrendered one taken-for-granted notion of reading, that it is limited to something someone does with a book. The first author I read who offered me a new view was Brian V. Street, a British professor who opened the introduction to his *Literacy in Theory and Practice* (1984) by writing, "I shall use the term *literacy* as a shorthand for the social practices and conceptions of reading and writing" (p. 1). The term *reading* was widening to *literacy* and began to include not only reading and writing, but math ("numeracy"), technology ("computer literacy"), and information literacy as well. The term also came to mean the contexts of school and beyond school where literate behaviors are learned and used. Jenny Cook-Gumperz (1986) summed up this entire set of assumptions about literacy and what it could offer, such as social mobility, by calling it "schooled literacy" (p. 2).

I was not alone in having thought for many years that writing rode piggyback on talk. For example, Roger Cayer and Renee Sacks (1979) wrote: "Of the two, oral language is primary and is acquired in a comparatively functional and natural way. Learning to write is a more formal and less natural endeavor" (p. 121). The emerging view, however, was that language forms, spoken or written, were differently suited to different functions.

A second major element of this new view was a sudden emphasis on the power and the prevalence of *dichotomies,* or the act of understanding an idea or entity through deconstructing it into mutually exclusive or contradictory entities. Everywhere I looked, authors were seeking the "binary oppositions which organize the flow of value and power" (Scholes, 1985, p. 4). Scholes's *Textual Power: Literary Theory and the Teaching of English* (1985) explored territory important for classrooms like mine as well as for the broader English profession. Like Goodman and Goodman, he observes that his own view of theory is in fact grounded upon teaching (p. ix).

As Scholes (1985) described it, a useful approach to analyzing dichotomies first locates central oppositions surrounding a particular issue or institution. It then lays each of the oppositional terms bare, and critiques (or deconstructs) each side of the opposition. In that way, he says, we dismantle "the way things are." Once a new and better direction is envisioned, we can move toward "consequential action." In this way, Scholes uncovers the "invisible apparatus" that divides professors of literature from composition professors. All English teachers can assist in dismantling and reconstructing some disquieting social practices in our field (pp. 10–17).

Newly alerted to dichotomies, I recognized the contradictions in my own institution, in my profession, in college-level versus remedial-level instruction, in the "skill versus whole language" debates, and even in my own ways of teaching literacy. Is reading a private act, a social act, or both? Is the point of reading to listen to the author, or to ignore the author for the text? Are comprehension and composition taught or simply learned by doing?

Literacy as a Transformative Act

One of the major research shifts I encountered had to do with the purpose, or function, of reading. In earlier research, the stated purpose of reading was to understand either the author's message or the message of the text that a close reading can reveal. But in *Beyond Communication: Reading Comprehension and Criticism* (1990), edited by Deanne Bogdan and Stanley B. Straw, the contributing authors probed language and literature as literacy "beyond communication."

What does it mean that literacy goes beyond communication between reader and author or reader and text? These researchers view literacy as transformative, a self-actualizing act. This line of thinking is in contrast with the idea of reading as communicating "a message in a bottle" from an author or the hidden theme in a text. Instead, "the purposes of reading—actualization rather than communication—have been radically changed from an interaction point of view. . . . The locus of meaning is identified with the reader" (Bogdan & Straw, 1990, p. 87).

A similar view was expressed in Myron Tuman's *Preface to Literacy* (1987), a sadly neglected book. He argued that a reader began as a person with certain kinds of qualities, belief systems, and values, and that through the act of reading, some aspect of that reader becomes changed, transformed (pp. 23–25).

Of course the self-actualization view did not wait to appear until after the communication models had their day. It had its beginning in the transaction model of Louise Rosenblatt (1983), a high school and university teacher who saw reading as a dialog or *transaction* between readers and text. By *transaction*, Rosenblatt meant "the interrelationship between the knower and what is known" (p. 27). Rosenblatt emphasized how the personal and aesthetic reactions of readers make meanings and individual knowledge. She says, "No one can read a poem for someone else. . . . The reader of the poem must have the experience himself" (p. 33). She did not regard other kinds of reading, such as instructional manuals or schoolbooks, in the same way. She writes, "We rarely object to a summary of a biology text" (p. 33).

Three decades after Rosenblatt's volume was first published in 1938, Stanley Fish also argued in opposition to the long-revered belief that texts contain a single message. Fish's best-known collection of essays, *Is There a Text in This Class?* (1980), builds on a particular dichotomy: Is meaning in the text, or is meaning located in the reader's interpretations? Fish maintains that even though everyone may have in hand a book with the same title, there is nevertheless no single text. Instead, he says each reader constructs from the text the meaning most relevant to his or her wants and needs. During his pondering of these ideas over 10 years, Fish determined that what is "real and normative" in literary works are the multiple "ways of reading" arrived at by a particular interpretive community (1980, pp. 317, 333–332).

Literacy as a Social Construct

The previous rush of research had sought the universal structures underneath languages. In this new wave, ideas of meaning and knowledge changed. The recognition of fragmentation, of many meanings, and of more local and fewer global principles than had been thought replaced searches for universal structures of mind, language, or meaning.

Andrea Lunsford (1991), author of college textbooks as well as major research publications, states the shift: "Systems of knowing are not givens . . . but rather are themselves composed [or constructed, to use the term of choice]; . . . only by actively composing our worlds can we know them" (p. 9).

Fish (1980) echoes Lunsford's social constructionist view, but with a focus on reading rather than composition: "Interpretation is not the art of construing but the art of constructing. Interpreters do not decode poems; they make them" (p. 327). The means by which readers make texts are "social and conventional; . . . the 'you' who does the interpretive work . . . is a communal you and not an isolated individual" (p. 331). Thus it became widely accepted that literacy is socially constructed.

Schooled Literacy

Rhetoricians, literary critics, teachers of English, and other humanists and social scientists were suddenly speaking of reading and writing as requiring similar "procedural knowledge" and as similarly collaborative. While both composition and reading had been seen as private and isolated acts, the social constructionists saw both as centered in collaboration. Kenneth Bruffee, a professor who taught composition at various levels, argued that the faces of learning and of composing change when writing classrooms become structured around students talking, reading, and writing together. In a bibliographic essay, Bruffee (1986) brought together "constructionist texts" to reveal them as part of a "coherent school of thought" (p. 773). According to James Petraglia (2000), Bruffee's notions of social learning can be traced to Vygotsky. Other social constructionists like James Berlin, Petraglia says, grounded their notion of socially constructed literacy in the radical pedagogy of Paolo Freire (Petraglia, 2000, p. 99).

There was one other important approach to literacy that concerned itself less with what teachers said about learning to read and write and more with how classroom procedures contributed to inequities in learning. To address some "hidden agendas" in cultural transmission, Jenny Cook-Gumperz edited a volume entitled *The Social Construction of Literacy* (1986). Trained in the social sciences rather than the humanities, the editor and authors of this volume did not define "social construction" in quite the same way as Kenneth Bruffee or Stanley Fish did. Instead, Cook-Gumperz collected articles by researchers in order to "focus on the processes by which literacy is constructed in everyday life, through interactional exchanges and the negotiation of meaning in many . . . contexts," primarily classrooms (p. 2).

The articles in Cook-Gumperz's publication all point to a central conclusion: Literacy mastery—or the failure to acquire such mastery—is not necessarily dependent on birth, race, or social status, as John Ogbu had argued. Instead, *schooled literacy* is influenced by interactions over time: informal judgments, learning-group behaviors, standardized tests, and "all the other evaluative apparatus" of schooling (Cook-Gumperz, 1986, p. 2). For example, one contribution (Collins, 1986, pp. 117–137) showed how problems develop in reading achievement in 1st-grade reading groups when disorderly turn taking interrupts lessons. Another study (Simons & Murphy, 1986) of one child's effort to describe a hidden object to a partner seems symptomatic of the first child's difficulties with school writing.

In the view of researchers who collect and analyze interactions, school failure does not happen because of a single test failure or by some mechanism of social determinism. In their view, school success or failure is in part constructed by interactions among teachers and the students in their classes; many small misunderstandings or successes pile up on one another. Over time, teachers' interpretations add up to evaluations of the student's ability and willingness to learn (Cicourel, 1974, p. 2). This, in turn, affects grades, placement in skill-based reading groups, and promotion to the next grade (Leiter, 1974, pp. 17–73). As I understand it, the effects of daily interactions—be they in the learner's favor or not—constitute the profound meaning of the phrase *social construction*.

In Response: A Place of My Own

I had spent a lifetime reading and half my life thinking about reading: how to teach the reading/writing processes, what literacy does for us, and what literacy means. Through many small, regular acts of attention, I had—in Gertrude Stein's words—gained "familiarity" with the subject. Stein (1935) defines the essence of familiarity in terms of appreciation: "I could look at any oil painting. I looked at any and at all of them and I looked at thousands and thousands of them" (p. 78). Just as Stein had looked at thousands of paintings in order to gain an appreciation for the art of painting, I had looked at many kinds of reading in order to learn how to appreciate the act of reading. Stein's words about the act of appreciating spoke to me about my process: forming and re-forming questions, experimenting, feeling "bothered," and commencing again. Of course the subject of reading allowed many possible ways of defining and describing the acts of reading. From the possible, I had to select my own essential parts.

I came then to view most reading as transformation rather than communication. Author and reader together build the best version of meaning making. As others have noticed, readers no less than writers compose meaning. Louise Rosenblatt and Stanley Fish had reminded me not to seek a single "right" interpretation, a single intended message from a distant author, or a single moral from the text. Instead, as Fish (1980) said, readers take on the "interpretive community's" perspective to create a satisfactory reading of any particular poem or story. However, the literary critic Stanley Fish and the literacy teacher Smokey Wilson did not share an "interpretive community." His literacy interpretations emerged from those who analyzed Milton—that is, from a "true reading" that was accepted and appreciated by others in his circle. His community was certainly not mine, nor was it the marginalized readers in an urban 2-year college classroom.

I had assumed Fish was the master builder of a social construction model where the reader constructs a reading either alone or in working with others. However, as I read more closely, I changed my mind. I had admired him as a spokesperson in democratizing school-based reading, but in fact, the poet John Milton's life and work was Fish's major focus, and most of his views were confined to literary criticism. My students and I did not concentrate primarily on literary works. Both vocational and academic majors found themselves involved in (or overwhelmed by) an array of texts—from sociology to computer science. But these texts, too, can have a transformative power. Darleen had found English "fascinating," but I believe it was the act of grasping the meaning and structure of text, the awareness of her own learning, that became awe-inspiring and fascinating. Students need to become familiar with texts by having access to works that engage them, that speak to them about important themes of their lives. But, as rhetoricians were arguing, it is also important to consider purpose, audience, and subject matter. Introducing the wide field of reading is part of the academic invitation.

As a teacher of reading and writing, my focus was on how learning and success happened in classrooms. Work by John Gumperz and Jenny Cook-Gumperz and those who worked with them was built upon the possibility of social change. Theory about the transmission of literacy made no sanguine promises, of course, but social change held a place in that theory.

At the same time, my interest went beyond. It led me to ask how successful learning happens for those who have found school to be a frustration and a disappointment. How does the teacher transmit literacy? Readiness counts. Beyond that, I could find no steel-wrapped instructional reading sequence. I personally borrow from Robert Scholes's (1985) demand for one central approach: Stop "teaching literature" and start "studying texts." Until readers become engaged with texts, teaching others to locate facts or name literary devices makes no sense. Scholes's approach, on the other hand, makes great common sense to me. "Students who come to us now exist in the most manipulative culture human beings have ever experienced," he says. Couple this dangerous setting with their lack of "historical knowledge that might give them perspective on the [manipulators] that they currently encounter," and there is a need for teachers who will "enable them to make sense of their worlds, to see through manipulations of . . . texts," and to express responses appropriately. He recommends that students "not be reverent before texts," but "critical, questioning, skeptical." He recommends that we see reading and writing as "complementary acts that remain unfinished until completed by their reciprocals," so that we finish reading by jotting down responses to it and finish those responses by reading them over (pp. 15–16).

Scholes (1985) speaks of three related skills—reading, interpretation, and criticism—as being inseparable but distinguishable. *Reading*, he says, requires knowledge of the codes at work in any given text. As we read a great many narratives, we learn the code expressed through the genre of stories. Given a grasp of the genre, a reader can construct a whole world from a few indications. Any disturbance in the building of this world—any gaps or sense of incompleteness on the reader's part—activates processes of interpretation. *Interpretation*, Scholes (1985) says, is an activity that "depends upon the failures of reading. It is a feeling of incompleteness on the reader's part that activates the interpretive process" (p. 22). When a text uses a word the reader does not know, or hints at a level of meaning that is not yet obvious, the reader infers from what is written on the page to what is meant but has not yet been said explicitly. Interpretation is considered to be a higher-order thinking skill than just gathering facts. Interpretation is deciding what the facts mean, an act schools (and literary types) privilege highly. We *read* a parable, Scholes goes on to say, but we *interpret* its meaning. Interpretation then can lead to *criticism*—or critical thinking—which takes us beyond the merely personal or merely literary. Scholes suggests we can apply our human, ethical, and political reactions to the themes developed in a given fictional text.

In Retrospect: Catching Literacy from a Teacher

In so many ways, Scholes describes the kind of reading instruction I most admired: where the reader is active enough to know what is important about the unfolding text and is aware of how to move smoothly to interpretation and criticism. In barest outline, Darleen and I had engaged in a kind of reading where I was not asking questions to check her comprehension. Instead, we were reading together, that kind of bookish intimacy I had long sought. We were doing it, moreover, in a class of 30. It reinforced for me a sense of literacy flowing between two readers through newly permeable membranes–not too different from my sense of collaboration with Anthony after long minutes of struggle. I had been waiting for something, maybe a clearer understanding of the links between spoken and written language, between talk and literacy. Anthony and Darleen, caught in the act of learning, gave me a taste of what I'd been looking for. After that, my focus was on finding a way to clarify, both for myself and others, the process of the transmission of literacy from teacher to student.

Chapter 6

—

Gloria and Ruth: Student–Teacher Interactions

Does interaction influence students' writing processes and their essay grades?

As I described in Chapter 5, I had gained much from pondering Darleen's reading. Shifting my focus, even briefly, from writing to reading had shown me how to see both reading and writing as part of the larger universe called literacy. But I had not untangled the relations between spoken and written language. I began to study student–teacher talk and its influence on writing.

IN PRACTICE

So far I had only a single instance of a moment in which talk between teacher and student changed the student's writing: My videotape of a tutorial session with Anthony showed me ways our collaboration helped shape the student's shift from a nonstandard, community-based verbal style to the beginnings of a written style. I saw him take a step toward academic literacy. More important, our work had not chased him away from school. He had not disappeared, as Kelly had. He had stayed.

My work with Darleen had shown me a way to use technology so as to make use of a one-on-one strategy while teaching a full class. The studies with both Anthony and Darleen had not been planned but were "improvised" in the way Fred Erickson (1982) describes *improvisation*: the intuitive moves of musicians in a jazz ensemble instead of following a written score.

But now I needed more than fortuitous tapes or serendipitous lessons. And so I began to plan a large-scale study, one that would examine patterns of interaction to discover key influences on writing. Looking for what happens between teacher and student, I expected to find these patterns in the interactive moment itself.

But first I needed a trial run so that I could see if my plan was workable. I thought tutor–student interactions were important to student success, but I could also think of other causes of success. I finally narrowed my list down to three of the most likely alternative explanations of student success or failure: reading achievement, reasoning style, and cross-cultural interaction. I tested the effects of these three variables in order to determine whether talk really was important to student success.

In the course of the subsequent conferences I set up with students, I also came to understand a new and central problem faced by inexperienced writers whose spoken language is several steps away from standard edited English: the difficulty in moving from nonstandard spoken language to written language. A colorful and rich spoken style—first high-pitched then low, an emphasis on a word by stretching the vowel or by rushing the pace—lost both color and drama on the flat surface of blank paper.

Linguists and anthropologists had noticed this problem and saw it as explaining the *why* of educational inequalities. But these scholars were not teachers. My perspective was different. I regarded this gap between talk and writing not as the end but as the beginning point of teaching. It is Vygotsky's zone of proximal development—the point at which the student can do, with help, what he or she could not yet quite manage alone—what I think of as a moment of growth.

For my study I chose to look at the tutor–student interaction that comes just before the first real composition of the semester. The student's writing on this occasion determines placement in the higher or lower level of the college's Project Bridge writing courses. The two bits of interaction I describe below, one with Gloria and one with Ruth, show what can go wrong and what can go right. These two interactions also provide clues in a search for *why*.

Gloria

Gloria arrived early for our appointment on a warm fall day. Young, strong, and vigorous, she seemed surprised when our meeting was informal, almost casual. We started talking about what she could write for her letter of introduction, and came to an agreement when I said something like, "That's good. Why don't you write about that?"

Now Gloria, even more than other students I have described in this book, used vocal modulations and nonverbal gestures and expressions to give her story drama—strategies that do not translate directly into written language. Linguists have developed a system of transcription marks to make possible a written approximation of the sounds of oral speech, and I use here a much abbreviated list of those marks to give a sense of her speech. Of the perhaps 20 subtleties of accent, tone, and rhythm, I've marked only 2 kinds of voice quality: relative stress and relative length of vowels. Both provide speakers with an avenue for emphasis, similar to the emphasis writers achieve with coordination, subordination, and modification. Lower-case letters (including the capital letter at the beginning of sentences) stand for the speaker's "usual" conversational tone of voice. An underline with lower case letters signals noticeable emphasis: <u>work</u>. Capital letters signal additional stress: WORK. To signal the most emphatic tone of voice the speaker uses, both capital letters and underlining are used together: <u>WORK.</u> A colon signals the preceding vowel is held longer than surrounding vowels (HO:T), while a double colon (SU::N) signals additional emphasis. The analogy is that a singer may sustain one syllable for 2 beats or 4 beats in contrast to the usual single beat. If necessary, additional information is placed in brackets.

In Gloria's case, these marks are particularly limiting, for much of her speech simply cannot be rendered in print. In general, remember that speech has various ways to convey the speaker's meaning and they all depend on contrast. That is, a word is stressed because it is louder, longer, or otherwise varied in relation to the other words in the utterance. Gloria seems to use "stretched" vowels and louder tones to add emphasis to her statements.

> SMOKEY: OK, so here we go. Let's just make sure that you have a good story started here. OK? What was your day [in Mississippi as a child] like?
>
> GLORIA: Hard work 'n . . . just a lotta <u>hard</u> work . . . ho:: t su:: n
>
> SMOKEY: Can you make a picture, can we really <u>SEE</u> that? What <u>IS</u> hard work?
>
> GLORIA: Hard work 'n . . . just a lotta hard <u>work</u> during the <u>day</u> out in the hot SU:N. . . . It's like you <u>OUT</u> there in that <u>HO::T SU::N</u>, picking cotton 'n <u>su:n</u> jus <u>bu::rnin</u> ya, 'n this SA::CK, something like, uh croaker sack but it's like jean, but it's white, uh, beige color.
>
> SMOKEY: Mm hmm . . .
>
> GLORIA: You put it over your shoulda like this, like a purse, you sack way back there, and you <u>PICK</u>in CO:TTON and puttin it in the <u>SA::CK</u> and then as you clean one cotton stalk you go on over to the next cotton stalk, when you finish that row of cotton you go on to the next cotton stalk . . . until your sack get full, then you have this big old, um, cotton, big ole truck where they weigh your cotton, then they have a little piece a paper and they write your name down how much cotton you done picked, and you go back . . . [words rapid and soft] and you would get up

before the SU::N come up and not leave out the field till the sun go DO:wn, say like nine hours or more.

The heat and the endless rows of cotton—Gloria's emphasis on the sun and repetition evokes the dreary routine she describes. One cotton stalk after another cotton stalk till the end of the row, then start another row, until the trip to the truck and beginning again. From it we infer the boredom and the exhaustion for this child. The story she tells is moving, but no less moving is how she tells the story.

I listened again and again to the recording she and I had made, until at last I understood the way of speaking. After trying to record the voice quality as if on a musical scale, I gave up in favor of simply identifying a few of her special qualities of voice with the transcription marks explained earlier.

Gloria and I concentrated on her farm experiences for almost an hour. Every time I tried to end the session—as when I said, "You've got a lot to write about now" at the end of the cotton-picking episode—she thought of something to add. As if she had turned to a blank page or indented a new paragraph, she began again. For instance, at one point, she mentioned the family garden, and I said, "Oh, a little garden?" She laughed condescendingly.

GLORIA: No, not little. Twenny [twenty] acres cotton, cucumbers . . . take 'em to, the, uh, cucumber, uh, factory, and we'd have maybe ten big rows of corn, plant corn, then we had to pull the corn . . . and okry [okra] and thirty rows of sweet potatoes and Irish . . .

The session went on much too long. I started interrupting her, trying to force her to commit to telling about working in the fields. She ignored me. The more I pushed, the faster she spoke. Soon we were interrupting each other.

One memory led her to another, but I wanted her to focus on just one. When she finally stopped, it was almost the end of class. I encouraged her to stay and write her essay, but she was adamant about doing it at home. I was not surprised when I saw it was a list of farming duties, and the cotton rows were lost—no one to hear about them but me, no appearance in her writing at all. Only the long days remained:

When I was about 6 months old my mother left me whit my grand-mother in TuBolow Mississippi. And then when I troun 6 years old I had to go to work on the Form whit my gran mother from Monday to Friday we worked. And I had to pick cotton, milk cows, and rase a

garland [garden]. . . . We wold get up before the sun come out and go
to work and work when the sun go down our bathe Room was out
side we all so had to get out water come from a well or stream.

During the writing conference, I had felt overwhelmed by the deluge
of language and of fascinating memories. Many of them, like the killing of
a large snake as the family was working the garden, would have made a
striking essay. But I remembered Mark all too well. As with Mark, she and
I had not arrived at a focus that allowed her to write effectively the tales
she had to tell. As a lesson in the critical conversion of talk to writing, we
made little progress.

Ruth

At the same time, in a classroom next door, another pair was also at
work talking. The student was from Mississippi and not much older than
Gloria; the tutor was White, as I am, and experienced in working with this
group of students. What those two constructed is an example of the talk
ball caught midflight and reshaped (or recontextualized) for writing in the
best Vygotskian practice.

Again, it is important to attempt to read the recorded speech accurately—or at least as accurately as possible within the constraint of print.

> Tutor: [reading from student's brainstorming notes] Let's see what
> else we got here. "I like to talk about the old days in my family, the
> way I was raised." Do you think there's more you'd like to write
> about? When you were a kid?
> Ruth: I would LO::VE to. I HA:D did some writing on myself, on my
> father and the way he was raised. I really didn't complete it . . . it's
> a LO::NG STOrE: [long story] and he had so MA::NE: KIDS.
> Tutor: Can you think of any other stories about friends and family?
> An incident [that] sticks out—other incident you'd like to write
> about? Would you like to tell more about him?
> Ruth: I know he was uh old CRE::K Indian. He like to go around in
> the woods and gather these herbs.
> Tutor: Who? Your father?
> Ruth: My father, 'n he like to make his own medicines 'n he always
> had a quite GO::OD re:me:dies that he use for his family, that he
> never beLIEVED in takin his family AFter SICKness to the DOCtor
> to have 'em examined like anything happen to um, uh to the family
> he always had some thing he could use.
> Tutor: Some kinda herb?
> Ruth: Some kinda herb thing he could use to heal 'em.

TUTOR: Were you ever sick and did he ever use them on you?

RUTH: I <u>WERE</u>, once. I had this <u>FE</u>:ver I don't know exactly what <u>KI:ND</u> of fever it <u>WAS</u> but it happened to me when I was seven years old 'n uh . . . [interrupted]

TUTOR: Why don't you just tell me about [it], from the beginning? From when you were sick?

RUTH: When I was seven years old, I fell sick with a fever. It was a fever they called a romatic fever, some kinda lowland fever that it STRU::ck me but it kept me down about a WEE::k 'n my father he had something that they call uh old cow HORN he went in the woods to FI::nd that . . .

TUTOR: Umm [interrupts Ruth; tries for clarification]

RUTH: [ignores tutor] . . . after the time deceased a cow deceased a <u>CO::W</u> in the <u>WO:ODS</u> he would go out 'n get the horns from the cow body, a cow?

TUTOR: A car?

RUTH: you know like a cah, a C-O-W. A cow.

TUTOR: Ohh, ohh, okay.

RUTH: Like a OX you know, some kinda like they call it an old deer horn? And he would take em and roast em in the ashes, make a fire outside and roast the horns like 'n he would <u>stra:pe</u> [scrape] it 'n put it in so mucha water and so mucha herbs 'n he would boil it, and he give me tea from it. And my fever went away that same day he give me the medicine.

TUTOR: um hum . . .

RUTH: It jus' went away 'n I had been sick for <u>FI::VE</u> <u>DA:ys</u>.

TUTOR: Wo:w.

RUTH: 'N after discover the remedy of getting my fever down, then after that I got <u>U:P</u>.

The various strategies the tutor used in this conference that help the student transform spoken language into written mode became clear to me over time, everything from reordering the action so that it better fits written narratives to pronouncing words so that they could be found in a dictionary. I highlight these strategies, and others, in Chapter 9.

For now, it is enough to see how Ruth was able to put in writing what she had just talked through with her tutor:

I remember when I was seven years old. I took a Romic fever. I was sick For five days.

My father took A OXHORNE and screaped it in water and HERBS. And he give it to me to Drink it taste like when you go to a Dr and have a teeth Drill out. It give me a ALKA SELZER felling and

I stard sweating and I fealt good and go out are the bed and starded playing again in the afternoon.

Both Gloria and Ruth show a lack of familiarity with written conventions and must struggle in various ways to place the emphasis of multi-channeled story telling on a two-dimensional page. Similar in background and working equally hard in the conferences, the central contrast between them is the difference in outcome. Gloria's writing has no focus beyond "farm life," and no matter how her tutor sought such a focus during the writing conference, it was not achieved. Ruth's writing has a focus—"my father cured me in just one day"—and the outline of a narrative.

Given what we can infer about these two students from what we know of them, what are the chances of each for attaining school success? In some ways, they are similar. Both began the program with similar scores on a standardized reading test, placing at about the 6th-grade level. Both came from the rural South. Both use "ebonics" or African American Vernacular English (AAVE).

They are not similar, however, in the way they answered a reasoning task I tried, a task that Alexander Luria (1976) had used in his work with newly literate collective farmers in Uzbekistan. There are six syllogisms in the task, each ending in a question. One of the syllogisms is this:

> Gold is a precious metal.
> Precious metals never rust.
> Does gold rust, or not?

Does the student answer each of the six syllogisms in terms of the syllogism or in terms of personal experience? Alexander Luria found those who were more literate used the text to form their answers, those who were less literate used their experience. I anticipated more or less the same trends. Yet what I found was not what I expected.

Gloria, a less successful reader, answered all the questions using the text as evidence ("It says that precious metals don't rust, and gold is a precious metal"). Yet, Ruth, who is a stronger reader, answered all six questions by referring to her own experience and ignoring the written text. Her answer was "It stay the same, it never will rust because my mother she had a gold ring and it never changed." Ruth then reread the text and said "My experience, it never rusts."

Ruth relied on experience (in many ways a strength) but did not recognize the task of the moment—which was to hold what we know in abeyance and answer according to the text. Gloria did. She took one look at the page of questions and said in answer to each one, "The paper says so."

In other words, Gloria would seem to be better connected to the printed page, so essential to getting information outside personal experience and thus essential to academic success.

In fact, however, Gloria finished the first semester but never returned. When I tried to reach her, the phone had been disconnected. Ruth finished the entire basic skills program and then went on to receive her cosmetology degree. In the moment of interaction, tutor and student met exactly where the student was, and together they passed through talk to writing. I wondered what relevance (if any) these syllogistic responses suggested about the students. This one small study predicted what I would find in the larger study—successful interaction seemed a variable that outweighed other influences.

I wanted a lot of examples of this kind of talk, and of the writing that followed it. The next semester I asked four tutors to work with me. Out of all these exchanges, I hoped to gather somewhere between 30 and 50 conferences. Some would probably go badly, others very well, and, with luck, we would find many with those magic moments when we could actually see the transmission of literacy, the handoff of literate strategies from experienced writer to beginner.

In Theory: Social Construction Develops

Reviewing the work with Gloria and Ruth set my feet on solid ground. I had spent quite a while learning about the reasons for school failure that the social scientists had worked out and had concentrated on how literate behaviors were passed on (or not passed on) in American classrooms. Interested in theory rather than teaching, researchers had little to say about the methods teachers should use to support learning.

I was a teacher. I worked in a writing classroom. My major interest was in how the research I was doing would contribute to the teaching in those classrooms. Some of it I had thought through, but I had not traced the undercurrents of theories and methods that governed this field of composition studies: written products, composing processes, and studies of conflict and collaboration that shaped new ways of teaching basic writers.

Composition and Instruction

As I went about gathering data to learn more about talk and writing, I had an underlying sense of anxiety, confusion, and even dread. By relying so heavily on talk, my instructional approach was different from most of the composition instruction common in our schools. I emphasized *process in collaboration* over *product in isolation.*

To begin with the broadest perspective, the great debate centered on two views of teaching English. The first came to be known as the "current-traditional" (or "formalist" or "discipline-centered"). The other was called the "composing processes" (or "writing process") approach.

In the words of Richard Fulkerson, the current-traditional method emphasizes "the composed product, the analysis of the essay into words, sentences, and paragraphs; the classification of discourse into description, narration, exposition, and argument, and an emphasis on correctness": good writing is "correct writing at the sentence level"(quoted in Gere, 1986, p. 30).

By the early 1980s, however, the writing process movement was well established and had taken a front-and-center seat in the ways of teaching writing. Youngsters were encouraged to begin drafting with "free writing," as a means of idea generation or invention. They were then encouraged to write a rough draft, followed by revisions (usually after collaborating with a writing group or talking with a teacher), and then to edit or proofread an almost-final version. The process was spoken of as being recursive: That is, it could be repeated, from any stage, and for any part, of the writing. Thus students were sometimes asked to "free write" in order to strengthen a description in the third paragraph of a draft, or edit the first paragraph last. These instructional strategies allowed students to work out their own ideas. But sometimes students would sit for a long time before blank pages, and it is at this point that the collaborative approach becomes essential.

Origins: What Is English?

If one could pinpoint the beginning of a shift in English language classrooms from product to process, it would be found in the change in students' needs. As Patricia Bizzell (1986) pointed out, students bring to class essays that cannot be improved with just a few stylistic changes, as product-based English course had assumed (p. 51). Instead, instructors have to specialize in teaching and research about composing, especially the practices of those who are not expert.

As "English" began to be many different things to many different people, a 3-week seminar was held at Dartmouth in 1966. Co-sponsored by the National Council of Teachers of English (NCTE) and the Modern Language Association (MLA), the seminar sought to define English as a school subject. According to Joseph Harris (1991), who chronicled this conference, it was heralded as a major shift from treating English as something people *learn about* to a view of something people *do*.

James Britton argued that English is not a subject matter, but rather "that space in the curriculum where students are encouraged to use language in more complex and expressive ways" (quoted in Harris, 1991, p. 634), learning through the use of language—reading, writing, and talking about issues related to their own personal experience. A number of Americans embraced this perspective. In 1968, James Moffett presented *Teaching the Universe of Discourse* and with it influenced the teaching of writing in American colleges. Peter Elbow's *Writing Without Teachers* (1973) suggested that teachers simply needed to allow youngsters time to write without intervention. Donald Murray and his graduate students, mostly teachers like Nancie Atwell (1987), helped spread this pedagogical approach through publications and teaching other teachers. Jim Gray's Bay Area Writing Project, which gave rise to the National Writing Project, invited teachers to teach other teachers. And Ken Macrorie's highly successful text *Telling Writing* (1970) became a standard in many community college classrooms at the time.

But throughout these years, conflicts between traditional-rhetorical teaching, skill-based instruction, and writing-as-process classrooms continued. In courses more focused on literature, such conflicts intensified. E. D. Hirsch (1988, 2001) became a popular spokesman for "cultural literacy," a body of knowledge that everyone in American culture should understand. But exactly what was this knowledge? Was it a matter of memorizing facts and time lines? In discussing composition and literature, David Bartholomae addressed a primary issue: What constitutes knowing? In his introductory chapter to *The Teaching of Writing* (1986), a landmark publication by the National Society for the Study of Education, he gives two writing teachers as examples, both of whom teach Blake:

> The teacher who requires regular short papers from his students, who uses those papers for in-class discussions, . . . and who has students revise those papers makes the reading of literature something substantially different from . . . the teacher who gives lectures on Blake, gives two essay exams, and assigns a research paper due at the end of the term. (pp. 1–2)

The writing skills called for in the two courses are different, but, more to Bartholomae's (1986) point, "Blake is different." He says, "You 'know' Blake differently if you have recorded your impressions in a journal, summarized articles, or written short papers on specific textual problems." The second teacher in Bartholomae's example gives priority to accepted interpretations; the journals and short analytical papers that the first teacher assigns "value . . . problems or paradoxes that break the pattern of set interpretation or received knowledge" (p. 2). How instruction proceeds means students "know" Blake differently.

These composition battles were not trivial. They called into question the nature of knowledge and the kinds of knowledge high schools and colleges should teach and learners should have. Those who held to strengthening skills or to promoting national literature as a body of knowledge to be mastered found themselves often in conflict with the idea of language and literature as a major road to growth and understanding.

By 1986 the battle was far from resolved. Figures who were important in the field at both university and K–12 schools began to chafe under the writing-as-process techniques. Lisa Delpit (1986) argued that the needs of minority youngsters and the voices of their parents were ignored and silenced, that students from minority communities needed explicit instruction beyond "the writing process" in ways that children in mainstream homes may not require (pp. 21–23). Further, she argued, the writing process method was restricting students to an overload of personal-experience writing tasks, offering them too few opportunities to stretch their skills for using language as a means, an instrument, of knowledge making (pp. 12–18). In "The Four Uses of Language" in her book *The Making of Meaning*, Ann Berthoff shares her concern that youngsters must learn much more than personal experience writing (1981, pp. 119–126).

Studies in Cognition and Composing

During this time, I divided my study between collecting talk and writing samples from students and seeking a niche into which my research could fit. As I understood the various approaches to instruction, I turned to the studies that were being carried out during these 2 decades.

In composition research, those interested in cognition began to study what happens between the writer's mind and the marks on the page. Linda Flower at Carnegie-Mellon University used "think-aloud protocols," asking writers to verbalize their thoughts about what they were writing as they wrote (Flower, 1987; Flower & Hayes, 1981). Sondra Perl (1979) was one of the first investigators to apply this method to adult writers in basic writing courses. Interactions between writer and tutor, however, seemed of little or no interest to these researchers. In one study, Perl collected data on "Interacting with Others" but the data were later dropped from the analysis.

Studies such as these focused on what happens in people's minds as they compose in isolation. In general, there was agreement that talk was easy, writing was difficult. Speakers could receive feedback from auditors, but the writer was seen as "a lonely figure cut off from . . . listeners . . . [and] condemned to monolog" (Rosen, 1978, pp. 141–142).

As far as I could tell, little had been said about what inexperienced writers could do in collaboration with teachers or competent peers. I had been tracing what happens when teachers work collaboratively with inexperienced writers, especially with those whose ways of speaking were regarded as different or difficult. But my interest in collaborative interaction and writing seemed to go against the grain of the major thrust in composition research. In light of the work I had put in, I was concerned when it began to look as though my focus was veering toward a dead end.

Writing Conference Studies

Relieved, even thrilled, when I located research on writing conferences, I was reassured. These writing conferences were, of course, different from those I planned to study. For example, the conferences usually were scheduled after a writer's rough draft was ready for revision and evaluation, not during the moment of composition. But research into conferences brought my work in line with one of the central directions in composition and would reveal a new facet of composing processes.

These conferencing studies showed various ways of conducting tutorials. Sarah Freedman (1976), for example, emphasized that a writing conference was instructional. Others emphasized topic development or teachers' questioning or revision (Garrison, 1974; Jacobs & Karlinger, 1977). All these studies were pushing the inquiry away from writer-in-isolation and toward collaboration—the direction I wanted to pursue.

In Response: Constructing Writing Collaboratively

One thing was clear: Composition theory needed a study of writing processes as they were carried out in collaboration with students like mine— very inexperienced writers in urban areas all across the country, both in and out of high school, directionless and ill-prepared for the demands that college or work would make.

Looking back, I saw my questions had deepened over the years. When they had first started pursuing me, I had thought to take care of them easily by going back to graduate school where I expected the answers would have already been found. Instead, the educational psychologists' view of pathological culture and genetic deficits held center stage. Everything in my teaching experience had rejected that answer.

Then, almost at once, the field opened to include linguists, sociolinguists, and anthropologists trained as participant observers who had documented the differences between mainstream culture and what was called the Black subculture. Their insights were part of what I needed. Without these insights I might never have thought to look at conversations and miscommunication across ethnic boundaries and social class. I would not have understood that even teachers with the best intentions in the world can unintentionally be party to making school inhospitable. Nor would I have realized the extent to which images of teachers had been tarnished. From almost every perspective, in the views of many researchers, schools and their teachers were responsible for the chasm between the success of mainstream learners and the failure of learners of color.

The urban classroom is multicultural and replete with variety. Multiple ethnic and social backgrounds carry with them multiple rhetorical styles; students bring these to the classroom, and these styles provide the spice in this variety. They can, of course, influence student–teacher communication and students' writings as well. One thing the examples I have cited share is a style Deborah Tannen (1985) christened "high involvement": that is, involvement that assumes shared community knowledge and relies heavily on the listener knowing about "that place over there." And that is exactly what our diverse urban classrooms do not provide.

My own teaching experiences here make the point. Though I tried to pick up the rhythm, the proper intonation, the placement of encouraging comments, instructional interaction was not easy to calibrate across cultural and rhetorical styles. As a result, I miscalculated, and miscommunications occurred often, and talk went around the block instead of achieving its goal. The new wave of research on writing conferences gave me a tailwind. With growing interest in interaction, the conversations between teachers with students (or experienced student-writers with those less experienced) offered an ideal classroom setting to study.

Vygotsky's zone of proximal development provided a core idea of what to seek: observations of learners in the initial acts of learning to compose as they work with a more capable partner. Following Vygotsky's lead, I thought of this zone as the ground between teacher and student, a first and necessary meeting ground to help students acquaint themselves with written-style language that differs from their spoken language. Since both teacher and student must work interactively to inhabit that space where change takes place, it is no surprise that sometimes the talk does not go smoothly. But the reward from those times when it does makes a great deal of frustration worthwhile.

In Retrospect: Finding School Success

But now I wanted to push one step further, push beyond accounting for school failure. I wanted to show what school success looked like for students who statistically were expected to fail. I wanted to show that instead of assigning blame for the school failure syndrome, we needed learning and teaching strategies that teachers could use with the students who needed these practices the most. The Grail of my quest was to uncover such strategies whereby teachers could learn explicit ways to help students transform talk into written compositions.

At that point, I could not fully describe the strategies that accomplish this transformation. I had seen them in action, for something had happened with Anthony to make him a fluent writer; something had happened with Ruth to allow her to order her narrative and describe in detail her father's practices. I knew teaching is not magic, and that "caring" in a teacher is necessary but not sufficient. I had seen that literacy was contagious and that learners caught it from their teachers—and hoped soon to identify the strategies at the heart of this transfer.

Part IV

ANALYZING ARTIFACTS

The chapters in Part IV—"From Talking to Writing, From Questioning to Finding" and "Maybell: Moving Toward an Academic Identity"—illustrate two broad types of analysis.

The data in Chapter 7 have been approached quantitatively. Transcripts and essays were defined so that they could be scored; statistical programs used on these scores show correlations between kinds of talk and holistic writing scores.

The data in Chapter 8 have been approached qualitatively. Responses on a survey were analyzed to form groups from which two students were chosen for interviews. The discussion is based on what this information suggests about developing an academic identity.

When choosing the material that casts new light on the question, the researcher must also choose the appropriate analysis—whether numerical or verbal. Again, the "Guide" suggests a few kinds of studies that could be addressed from either quantitative or qualitative perspectives. As the talk and writing studied suggests, some combination of the two may be best.

Chapter 7
——

From Talking to Writing, From Questioning to Finding

What can converting research findings into practice tell us about school performance?

In the previous chapter, I described the human faces of students and tutors engaged in writing conferences. This chapter takes a longer view. It is a search for the contours or outlines in which individual faces become less distinct but patterns emerge–patterns of different kinds of communication among groups of students and teachers, patterns that allow for generalizations that can then be tested in other settings with other types of students.

RESEARCH INTO PRACTICE

What bothered me all along and led me to graduate school in the first place was the chasm between theory and research on one hand and classroom practice on the other. My major professors allowed me to base my dissertation on a quasi-experiment that I conducted in my classroom with students I knew well. When I finished the work described here, I could better understand how theory fit findings. I wanted to create a pipeline, a link that connects the classroom to the research university and the university to the classroom. What follows, then, is my take on the way anthropologists and linguists and psychologists can help us in the classroom.

An account of my research procedures can be found in my dissertation (Wilson, 1988). In this chapter I sketch only the questions I started with, the thinking behind the analysis, some illustrative evidence, and the findings.

THE STUDY: OVERVIEW OF ANALYSIS AND FINDINGS

In those basic writing classes where students are not comfortable producing more than a half page or so of writing, just how important is talk? My findings showed that smooth interaction between tutor and student is a crucial variable for about 20 percent of entering students in a basic skills program. Interaction is a more important variable than the students' reading ability, reasoning style, or the cultural backgrounds of those working together. Smooth interaction is useful but less central for another 20 percent. In other words, for every 50 students I saw, 10 depended upon talk with tutors to learn how to shift talk into writing, and 10 others wrote better essays because of their interaction with tutors. Twenty students in a group of 50—40 percent, or very nearly half an incoming class—needed to talk through an essay before composing it on paper. It is hard to put into words how important coming to that conclusion has been to me.

Over 2 years, I transcribed 51 tape-recorded conferences between tutors and students, each lasting about 1 hour. The eight tutors, of whom I was one, worked valiantly to assist students in their assigned composition task, and many students tried no less valiantly to write an acceptable essay. Finding a way to analyze these hours of talk was the first step.

Using the various kinds of exchanges between students and tutors, I devised a system for applying numbers to what I decided were meaningful interactive statements. In the end, I chose three kinds of evidence to quantify. First, raters assigned scores to how the tutor and student communicated: They scored the transcript of each writing conference, using contextualization cues to evaluate each turn as smooth or awkward. Second, raters used a separate scale to assign points to what the student said: whether or not a student's talk rehearsed a story in a style tutors regarded as appropriate for an essay to be written by an entering student in a basic skills class. Finally, raters used a conventional 12-point holistic score to evaluate the essays that students wrote after their talk with their tutor.

Preparing for Analysis

I hypothesized that the effectiveness of tutor–student interactions correlated significantly with the scores assigned to the students' essays. While a pilot study of a few students helps develop this kind of hypothesis, testing it demands over 30 samples. In this case, I had a data set of 50 writing conferences and an equal number of essays. I concentrated on three kinds of information gathered from these data: how student and tutor communicate (smooth or awkward interactions), what the student contributes toward the narrative to be constructed (the spoken contribution), and what the student writes after the conference.

The discussion of communication signals below is but a glimpse into the way the interactions were scored so that talk between student and tutor could be prepared for analysis. "Conversation" is qualitative evidence, and yet I wanted to show that overall, some kinds of tutor–student talk helped students compose essays, while other exchanges frustrated both tutor and student. I reached my findings by assigning numerical scores to the 50 tutor–student interactions. Since the findings depended in part on these scores, a glimpse into a few of the features used in the analysis will be helpful.

How Students and Teachers Interact

Identifying the features characteristic of smooth or awkward interactions was a critical task. After considerable study of conversations—both those I had collected and those analyzed by other researchers—I chose eight features that signaled whether a conversation went well or badly. I will discuss only the three most important features here, each a kind of linchpin on which the exchange either succeeded or failed.

John Gumperz (1981) theorized that speakers show they understand one another by the use of certain signals which he called "contextualization cues" (pp. 132–133). Deborah Tannen (1985) speaks of the same features and calls them indicators of "conversational involvement": They do not necessarily carry meaningful content, but they reassure speakers that "we're on the same page" (pp. 161–162). These cues or signals include the "yeahs," "uh-huhs," and nonverbal features such as rhythmic question and answers. Three examples of cues that are critical to the smooth unfolding of tutor–student exchanges include back-channel cues (responses from listeners that invite the speaker to continue), repairs of misunderstandings, and nonverbal (or paralinguistic) features (including vocal quality and gestures)—all ways in which speakers share conversational pace. When speakers do not share these means of signaling "I'm with you" to one another, it is immediately clear that they are not on a shared conversational track.

Back-Channel Cues. The placement of these signals—"uh-huh," "really?"—distinguishes smooth from awkward conversations. These are the stitches that indicate speaker and listener are creating a single conversation. Such cues can be strongly positive. When a student completes her narration, for example, a tutor can say, "Wow," "Great," "Perfect." These cues give the student confidence to follow the tutor's directions—"Write down that story just the way you told it." In contrast, when the student says, "So that's my story," and the tutor responds with a lukewarm, "Yeah, okay," the student may take that as meaning the story is not worth much and may change to a different topic entirely (and almost always an unsuccessful one).

Other back-channel cues, such as "uh-huh," "really," "huh," or "right," signal to the speaker that the listener is paying attention. The trick, however, is that these signals need to be placed precisely at the end of a speaker's comment or during a pause. If they come before, or after, they are interruptive.

Shared Meanings and Repairs. A measure of smooth interactions is the degree to which speakers share an understanding of key words. They may echo one another's words or phrases, as in Chapter 6 when the tutor, speaking of Ruth's fever, says, "he really cured you," and Ruth replies, "he really cured me."

Nonverbal, Prosodic, and Paralinguistic Signals. A "good conversation" is marked both verbally and nonverbally. Like dancers, speakers who share contextualization cues move in rhythm with one another, responding to each other's contributions right on time. Prosodic and paralinguistic features—the former refers to pitch, loudness, duration, and silence; the latter to what is often called "tone of voice"—are described in detail by the linguist David Crystal (1976), and refer to the "range of vocal effects which have a conventional role . . . in English" (pp. 126–128). And these features, unlike vocabulary, are mastered within speech communities.

Two or more of these cues can be used in a single utterance. In part of the discussion not included in Chapter 6, Ruth and the tutor are chatting and the tutor says, "I read about the, uh, snake." The student responds with "right" (a properly placed back-channel cue) and elaborates on the tutor's comment: "Right, the, uh, . . . hundred-year old rattler." Listeners may not be clear what "snake" they are discussing, but the interacting pair has the same referent in mind. In analyzing these writing conferences, the above exchange, or turn, illustrates a "smooth" exchange.

Smooth interactions are based on shared terms, words, and ideas; cultural background can influence our stock of knowledge, what we bring to bear on something new. Across cultures, genders, even generations, there will be misunderstandings. I have never forgotten the big yellow car, the "Baratz," which I spoke of in Chapter 2. Years passed before I understood what Mark meant. Why had I not clarified the matter at the time? I did ask Mark, but only once. By the time I met Anthony, my unconscious rule that teachers should know everything and not show their ignorance had been broken, and I had learned to stay with it and say "I don't understand" as often as needed.

What the Students Tell: Spoken Contributions

Intimately connected with kinds of interactions are the students' spoken contributions. The student's spoken contribution—the oral rehearsal for the written composition, or what the student says in his or her conversation with the tutor—determines how that tutor–student conference influences composition scores. When I deleted from each writing conference transcript all tutor comments and questions, only the student's words remained. To evaluate this student talk, I devised a system to rate the students' spoken contributions.

The transcripts showed four kinds of spoken contributions. The first was the monosyllabic response: The student offers no more than eight or nine words in the course of the conference, composed mostly of single words in response to the tutor's questions—"Yes," "No," "I graduated," "last summer" (for similar examples, see Labov, 1972a, 1972b). These contributions were disjointed and far indeed from a narrative. The second sort consists of voluble talk that seems to jump around from topic to topic, linked by the student's private associations. This speaking style has been called "topic associating" or "topic chaining" (see examples in Michaels, 1986, pp. 104–109).

With the third sort, the student stays with a particular story line, but explains it in ways that cannot easily transfer to writing (as one student describes a fishing trip: "that pole say, 'Boom, <u>BO::M</u>' and I moved like <u>THIS</u> [gestures pulling fish from water]"). This style has been called "highly involved" and makes an effective oral talk, but gets its power from precisely the devices that do not easily transfer into written language, devices that disappear if one is not in the room. The fourth kind of spoken contribution has been called "message-centered." The message-centered contribution concentrates on a single topic, elaborating and explaining it in explicit verbal terms (see Michaels, 1986). I asked raters to divide the spoken contributions into the four categories suggested by the work of Michaels (1986), Gumperz (1981, 1982a, 1982b), and Collins and Michaels (1986), and to assign points to each. The monosyllabic contributions received 1 point. The topic associative contributions received 2 points. The single topic contributions which relied on "high involvement" with the tutor (e.g., those that relied on oral cues) received 3 points. The message-centered topics received 4 points. Working individually, three teachers sorted the spoken contributions into the 4 categories, came to consensus without discussion, and assigned and added up scores for each category.

What Students Write: Essays

The essays students wrote after the writing conference were the third kind of data. The scores raters assigned to each essay served as the "dependent variable," the gauge for whether or not interactions with teachers varied in relation to the scores on the two spoken dimensions.

FINDINGS FROM THE ANALYSIS

When the analysis was complete, it showed that 32 students interacted smoothly with their tutors. Of these, 25 interacted smoothly with tutors as soon as they began to talk. Another 7 started out unevenly, as Anthony and I had done long ago, and yet (again as with Anthony) by halfway through the session, something triggered a much improved interaction.

While 32 pairs constructed talk that eventually led to higher writing scores, 18 other students participated in frustrating and awkward exchanges with their tutors or, after a few minutes, the exchanges deteriorated and began to run into misunderstandings they could not resolve.

The kinds of interactions and composition scores were significantly correlated. ("Significant," in the context of statistical inference, means that the probability of a particular finding's being an accidental occurrence is less than 5 times out of 100 [p less than .05].) When interactions began (or became) smooth, students' writing scores were at the upper end of a 12-point scoring scale: 7.5 for smooth interactions, and 6.7 for interactions that became smooth. In contrast, when interactions began awkwardly, the essays received scores on the lower end of the 12-point scale, an average score of 4.3. Essays written after deteriorating interactions were scored only slightly higher (5.2).

The writing conferences that guide these students' writing seem informal, but their structure is actually highly predictable. Each writing conference follows a pattern. It begins with an opening that frames the talk (goal setting, indicated by something like the tutor's "Let's see. What have you been thinking about?"). It shifts then to probe for a topic ("Do you want to write about _____?"). Once a topic is agreed upon, tutor and student collaborate to build a personal experience ("Tell me about that") followed by elaboration ("Try to remember the details"). The telling and elaboration can extend for many turns, and at the end, the tutor makes a positive evaluation—something like "Oh, that's really good." Finally, conference closure is in sight: The tutor makes the assignment official as he or she restates explicitly the subject the student has agreed to put on paper ("Can you write about that, just like you told me?").

But not all conferences go along so smoothly, and by examining problematic ones it becomes clear in just how many ways school talk can go wrong. Tutor and students can misunderstand one another at any of the six major junctures; from "Tell me" to "details" can be a critical stumbling block.

The conversation between tutor and student is in serious difficulty if any one of these major structural elements is missing. Suppose, for example, the assignment is not stated, or does not evolve directly from the conversation. In these cases, the student writing will probably be brief and may be unrelated to any of the subjects mentioned during the conference.

Interactions that run aground structurally reveal serious communication breakdowns between student and tutor. As a rule, however, such major collapse can be traced to problems at the turn-by-turn level. That is, each time one participant expects the other to return the conversational ball in a certain way, and the other participant responds in unexpected fashion, an observer can hear the faint sound of a warning signal.

TUTOR: So that changed your life. What happened, that first day in jail?
MICKEY: Nothing, just eating and that's it.

The tutor directed the student to write more about the first day in jail; the student ignored the assignment and wrote a thoughtful but jumbled paragraph on the meaning of freedom. His insights could be developed; I personally prefer reading jumbled ideas to reading about a day in jail. But the point remains: The writing received a low evaluation score, and the student dropped out of school within 6 weeks.

While the mistakes at the main structural points are the most disruptive, understanding at a turn-by-turn level can improve (or worsen) the interaction. No matter where problems occur, if they are recognized quickly, miscommunications usually can be repaired. And one repair can change the quality of the interaction in ways that correlate with essays that receive higher scores. Moreover, these repairs (initiated usually by the tutor) are often a hopeful sign for future writings; they can signal a moment in which the student trusts the tutor, takes a risk, and is on the brink of trying something new with help that she could not do alone. Instead of a breakdown that could have tipped the interaction toward the student's disengagement with the writing task, the conversational save—an "Oh, I see; that's good!"—can strengthen tutor and student rapport and even lead the learner to discover a new way to communicate in school. All of this sets the stage for the acquisition of new techniques for communicating in school settings in both talk and writing.

What determines how writing conferences proceed? Miscommunication has been blamed on differences in conversational style. But my evidence suggests that the ethnic backgrounds of the student and the teacher are *not* directly responsible for awkward communications. Problems emerge when students and teachers share different communication goals and these differences are not recognized or acknowledged. Tutors and teachers who are familiar with writing classrooms—many spending years helping students compose—have particular expectations about what constitutes an "appropriate" topic and development of a narrative essay for basic writing. When a student's talk violates the tutor's school-based expectations, the conversational going is (or becomes) tough sledding.

Smooth and developing interactions, those with few misunderstanding and with repairs rarely needed, most often co-occurred with message-centered or single-topic, high-involvement spoken contributions, which received 3 or 4 points, respectively. The average score for spoken contributions constructed in these rhetorical styles was 15.4 or 11.5. Awkward interactions that became smooth were only slightly lower than interactions that were smooth throughout. The most important feature of talk that led to a higher score on an essay was the single-topic spoken contribution, I concluded. The final chapter of this study shows in detail how tutors helped students adjust gestures and nonverbal comments to fit written language.

Much less positive are the outcomes for those students who were part of awkward or deteriorating interactions. These students' spoken contributions were, on average, assigned low scores. For awkward interactions, those in which almost every exchange was answered with no more than a word or two, the spoken contribution scores averaged 6.6—less than half as high as scores assigned to smooth, message-centered interactions. Some interactions quickly deteriorated into fits and starts, long pauses, or misunderstandings. In these cases, the students' spoken contribution scores were only slightly higher (8.0) than those involved in interactions that were awkward from the beginning.

Most of these low scores were assigned to certain kinds of spoken contributions. The monosyllabic offerings and those in which the student topic-chains (e.g., jumps from one subject to another) received the lowest scores of all. And there were distinct correlations between low-scored talk and awkward or deteriorating interactions.

These findings support the notion suggested long ago by several authors in Jenny Cook-Gumperz's *Social Construction of Literacy* (1986): Teachers and tutors expect message-centered talk, or, at the least, a topic-centered spoken contribution. When the student says little or nothing, or seems to change topics in every other breath, the teacher or tutor begins to attempt to get the "right" kind of story, and interactions break down. Unless the tutor and student can negotiate a shared idea of what subject is appropriate for an essay, the interaction then begins to go badly—and can go very wrong indeed—ending with just a "yes" or "no" from the student.

CHECKING OTHER VARIABLES

I assigned great importance to kinds of interaction. Logically, though, what if there are other differences in the students (or in the tutors) that are really responsible for the apparent importance of writing conferences? Would not better readers make better writers? In fact, reading achievement, reasoning style, interactions with tutors, the nature of students' spoken responses, and essay scores were interrelated in interesting ways.

Tutors had difficulty with the 14 beginning-level readers (grade level of 3.5). These students used a reasoning style that was usually based on personal knowledge and not on the text. Their oral narratives were generally composed of one- to two-word responses, their interactions with tutors were awkward, and their essays received the lowest scores. In contrast, the 19 most competent readers (grade level of 8.9) provided message-centered narratives, their reasoning style was inevitably text-based, they interacted smoothly with their tutors, and their essays received the highest grades.

These findings were predictable. The outcomes for the 17 students who had an average reading level of 6.4 were not. For these students, success or failure depended heavily on what happened between the student and the tutor. When—as with Ruth in Chapter 6—these mid-level readers had smooth interactions with their tutors and constructed topic-centered narratives in collaboration with their tutors, their composition scores equaled the scores of the most competent readers.

Most important, even though it seemed counterintuitive to me, it was possible to demonstrate statistically that the ethnic backgrounds of the students and tutors, shared or not, made no significant difference in the scores for either writing conferences or written essays. Still, even though shared ethnic backgrounds were not statistically important, there were several writing conferences in which it was obvious that awkward interactions were avoided by tutors' references to a shared African American background, particularly when both student and tutor came from the southern United States.

What it all added up to is that talk is crucial for particular kinds of students in schools. Teachers and tutors must know how to guide and develop such talk. Nothing, of course, is guaranteed, but a great deal hinges on how well the tutor and the student manage to create between them a conversation helpful to a writing task.

IN RESPONSE:
LITERACY QUESTIONS IN LIGHT OF THESE FINDINGS

In the 1950s and 1960s, university educators had walked the single path of the deficit and disadvantage theories, which proposed that some (White) people have an average or higher IQ while others (mainly people of color) do not. Those arguments lay miles back there on that path, preserved in the dusty publications of the last century. Since then, a dozen research avenues had been opened: studies of how power, society, schooling, and politics relate; studies in the analysis of language and of literacy; studies of technology and rhetoric/composition. Theories proliferated, and researchers turned away from a single, simple answer.

And just as my questions deepened over the years of study, so, too, answers unfolded. Looking back, I could consider how some educators' negative attitudes toward African American students seem to be linked to three major themes that have been with us from the first: the nature of literacy, the workings of conversation (or how people understand one another's meaning), and the relations between spoken and written language.

Each of these themes has been interpreted in the most negative perceptions of African Americans: Lack of literacy equates to lack of intelligence, nonstandard speech, and oral (for which read "primitive") culture. Such tacit assumptions, of course, affect school learning for people of color, particularly (but certainly not limited to) African Americans.

The Nature of Literacy

From the early 1960s until the mid-1980s, a common belief was the idea that literacy transforms the mind (Goody, 1977). It was more than a decade before Sylvia Scribner and Michael Cole (1981), two psychologists studying literacy among the Vai tribe in Liberia, challenged this assumption. After testing many general hypotheses, they concluded that literacy per se had no "general cognitive consequences" (p. 158). Instead, they discovered multiple literacies, and showed how specific uses of text strengthened various particular thought processes. For example, they found scholars of the Qur'an were adept in critical reasoning, perhaps because they had for many years practiced making fine semantic distinctions in order to interpret the words of the Prophet. A different set of functional cognitive skills appeared among those skilled in using literacy for other purposes. Readers of Vai, a native writing system, showed skills at auditory integration, for Vai script requires the exercise of this faculty.

My own work supports the notion that literacy function informs cognitive achievements. Kelly's literate abilities were adequate for his activities outside of school. But others like Anthony and Darleen had mastered various kinds of school literacies. Correlations between literacy and specific cognitive habits of mind, remember, are speculative: We have no information suggesting whether cognitive achievements modify with increased literacy use.

The linguist James Gee (1991) calls literacy a "socially contested term." By this he means that any definition of *literacy* carries with it a theory. A definition that focuses on "the ability to read and write" locates this ability in the individual, and the individual who fails is either culprit or victim. The problem with this individual-ability stance, taken prototypically by the deficit theorists, is that it "rips literacy out of its sociocultural contexts" and "obscures the multiple ways in which literacy interrelates with the workings of power" (p. 22).

Researchers like Shirley Brice Heath (1983), Brian Street (1984), Mike Rose and Glynda Hull (1990), and James Gee (1991) identified many literacies and began speaking of the "new literacy studies" (Gee, 1991, p. 39). In my own mind, literacy is a sociopolitical reality, far more and other than an individual intelligence's decoding and encoding words to make sentences.

Literacy is power. Literate persons, as the owners of this resource, are often seen as more powerful than illiterate ones. Those who face school as adults, at perhaps age 34, taking basic skills courses, are anxious to acquire educational power of their own. Although education may not result in immediate economic benefits, for some there still seem to be immediate and positive personal consequences. In Chapter 1, Rose could help her children with homework and also was able to regard herself as a successful reader and writer. Anthony, who began basic skills classes still "drawing" his letters, produced journals and stories of three or four pages by the end of a year. For others, I have collected considerable anecdotal evidence that basic skills courses are steps to economic stability as they provide the credentialing needed for better jobs. While this is not the capital-P "Power" Gee speaks about, it still is power within the personal realm, the power of setting a goal and achieving it, the power of self-respect.

Literacy, then, is power—both in the public arena and, at least in part, in the personal one. Collaboration actively fostered Anthony's ability to write a narrative (and, over the next three semesters, to write many more narratives). It also fostered Darleen's ability to read and, soon enough, to be able to read and respond to poems and articles about people different from herself.

In this context, the study of literacy has two faces. The political face invites researchers to look in the direction of the forest-as-a-whole: the political and cultural reality. The social face, personal at the same time, looks at a few trees in the forest: the community of teachers and students who see each other regularly, the small-scale interactions and behaviors of participants. Both large-scale and small-scale views are important. In fact, it seems that large-scale issues best come into focus by looking at them from a small-scale viewpoint.

Classroom Conversation

I have written much throughout this volume about the nature and effects of conversation on the writing of some students; the unfolding of this research is detailed in Chapter 4, which describes the move in research from abstract structures to languages in everyday life—from sentence and syntax to discourse and pragmatics.

I have emphasized—even belabored—this process, this move, because of a persistent negative judgment I kept hearing about the students I work with: "The problem is with the way they talk." If I selected one of the stereotypes most difficult to erase, it would likely be this complaint about the language of African American students. No matter what we learn from linguists like William Stewart, John Rickford, and Raven McDavid about dialects and language varieties, this perspective of a deficient language had been locked solidly into place by 1970 and persists today. Yet we knew little about the ways of speaking that African American enclaves practiced at home and brought to the classroom.

In my experience, schools, which supposedly set out to teach youngsters what they did not know, often had been an arena that, knowingly or not, devalued these children's oral language. I had observed how tutor and student managed casual-appearing conversations. I found no simple direct link between Black English and poor school performance.

A method selects its researcher, depending on the questions nearest to the researcher's passion. A study by Frederick Erickson (1976; see also Erickson & Schultz, 1982) started it off for me. Erickson videotaped counseling interviews in community colleges. He found that academic counseling was central to the aspirations of first-generation college students, that these interactive sessions either furthered or limited the course of students' goals and aspirations. The first mention of the term *gatekeeping*—referring to the ways institutions function to invite some learners in and keep others out—came from publications based on this study (Erickson & Schultz, 1982). While some of the counselors apparently were not rude to students, they did not necessarily show the students the path to advancement. In this way, oral language can block students from invitations to academia.

I recognized that writing conferences, like counseling interviews, were key encounters that carried more import than either student or tutor probably realized. In general, the more successful students were more able to follow their tutors' cues—especially if they were able to hit the target even when the tutor (unintentionally, no doubt) changed it unexpectedly. How were some able to manage the conversational moves that school talk demands, while others—similar in all obvious respects—were not?

Much of the approach I finally came to use is summed up in an article John Gumperz published in 1981, "Conversational Inference and Classroom Learning." This approach promised to explain how it could be that, in spite of overwhelming social barriers, many minority students do quite well while others in similar circumstances do not. As he put it, "We need to know how . . . cultural, political and economic factors interact with teaching strategies to affect the acquisition of knowledge and skill" (p. 4).

I learned from my study that some tutors welcomed their students into the academic enterprise, giving them many hints and tips about how and what to write. Others were unable to engage the students, and their interactions made little headway in developing the student's school performance.

But a teacher might ask, "What can I do in the classroom today, tomorrow?" If I had to choose one feature that will do the most toward inviting the student into the student–teacher conversation, I would choose in-the-moment conversational repairs. A corrected misunderstanding is the first step a teacher can take to move past a formal and institutionalized relationship with those who most need simply to be heard.

Spoken and Written Language

Most elusive of the three themes–and the most affected by distorting assumptions—is the relation between talk and writing. Had I not remembered Robert Scholes's (1985) warning about the power and prevalence of dichotomies, I might have made the mistake of viewing spoken and written language as opposites and never have come to terms with their kinships and overlappings. Worse, I might have remained angry and powerless against the scholarly charges of an "oral" culture as quaint, exotic, and illiterate.

For centuries, only written language was lasting enough to examine. But once anthropologists moved into the field—into distant Bali or among remote Inuit tribes, into the cultures where communication happened person-to-person—the study of oral languages became important. Consequently, when researchers began to look at spoken language in a world where writing was everywhere, they could no longer regard written language and oral language as being in simple either-or opposition. So how are written and oral language related? The dominant belief has been that spoken language is the base of written language. This view has been written in stone, and that, perhaps, is why I have had such a hard time thinking beyond it.

For the last 30 or 40 years, the assumption has been that oral language is primary, acquired naturally, and that writing is more formal and less natural, as Cayer and Sacks wrote in 1979 and as Louisa Moats echoes in 2001. Moats's article is paired with one by E. D. Hirsch (2001), and together the articles deal with overcoming the language gap. They state succinctly both the theme—the connections between talk and writing—and its distortion—that the problems people of color have in their spoken language lead to a lack of literacy. That is, their primitive oral culture keeps them from writing and reading and (perhaps) thinking. Their first three years in school are spent primarily on decoding, and, as Moats describes, they do well through 3rd grade. But then, because they do not know vocabulary, test scores drop and gains disappear. There is something wondrously circular in all that, but rather than taking up that argument directly, I began to look at the relation between spoken and written language in another light. In 1966, R. I. Allen wrote that "written English is one of the systems of English—a separate dialect, if you will—with its own rules, its own conventions, its own signals" (p. 383). For my dissertation study, I took Allen's position as my own, realizing that, although spoken language may be the basis of written language, writing is a separate and distinct variety of language with its own structures and functions. Furthermore, written language today represents a prestigious way of knowledge making. While the "language gap" view is global and unbridgeable, the "rules, conventions, and signals" view is specific and teachable. I am not saying that it is easily teachable. At this point, where research ends and teaching takes over, teachers know how hard-fought the struggle to convey a writing convention can be. Glynda Hull (1986) has pointed out in almost all her writings that written language rules, like computer software programs, can be "buggy." Students can internalize some rules without attention to other, overriding rules (p. 208). If a child moves, say, five times in her first three school years, why should we be surprised when writing conventions come to her a little "buggy"? She caught only parts in the first place, and by 4th grade (or maybe 6th), if these practices have not become habitual, they may not internalize quickly (Halliday, 1985).

Spoken and written languages have developed distinctive differences. Those who have teased apart these differences itemize important features. As Halliday (1985) says, spoken language as used in conversation makes clear its meanings in two ways:

1. Intonation: the raising and lowering of voice; for example, the placement of the strongest rise or fall (or "tonic prominence") in English is a "full stop," a grammatical feature.
2. Rhythm: the stressed syllables in an utterance, as the following sentences show: "There may' be ma'ny of these stressed syl'lables in one' stretch of lang'uage. There' can' be' few.'" (pp. 46–51)

It is almost impossible to reproduce talk in writing without a set of transcription rules. Most of the students' narratives in this book, like Gloria and Ruth's, lose the power they had in the telling when they are written down. It is tone and rhythm—along with other prosodic signals such as nonverbal facial expressions, hand gestures, dramatic role-playing to enact voices—that give spoken language its dynamic flow—a "sequence of small crescendos," as Halliday describes it (1985, p. 55).

Just as I have oversimplified the complexity of spoken language, so I oversimplify Halliday's definition of written language. It is, he summarizes, lexically dense, with a high information load in each clause, head nouns centrally important in clauses, adjectives or verbs changed into noun forms, and clauses signaling sequencing and relationships. While some occasions can be handled in either spoken or written language—questions to the teacher, for example—others, like research papers, do not lend themselves to spoken language.

Speakers of African American Vernacular English must be clear not only about the spoken dialect of talk but also about shifting into the written dialect in classrooms (Halliday, 1985, pp. 44–45). At one point in my work with John Gumperz, he published an article with Kaltman and O'Connor (1984) discussing the transition to literacy. They pointed out how the speech of highly literate adults contrasts with that of less experienced reader-writers. Selecting from the same exchange I described with Anthony, Gumperz chose a few lines at the end of the dialog. In this portion, Anthony is describing his "so-called friend" in a way, Gumperz said, that could not transfer to writing:

> Cool dude, you know, catch women, this and that, but he must get his no:se wide open behind some other girl, and this and that, and . . . lay up in the crib and rip me off

To turn this talk into writing, Anthony would have had to change key terms ("cool dude," "crib"), place them into full sentences, and remove the fillers ("this and that," "you know"). His community-based sayings, like "get his nose wide open behind," must shift into the register of mainstream classroom talk. Gumperz and his colleagues concluded that this kind of spoken language lacks the cohesive devices that will allow a reader to follow the written language. This observation makes a valuable theoretical point, especially when compared (as Gumperz shows) with the talk of graduate students. But here goals of researcher and teacher diverge.

Rather than illustrating the cohesive devices that are not yet in a student's repertoire, a teacher finds it more revealing to see what is almost internalized, Vygotsky's "buds of development" that can flower when assisted by a trusted other. In Anthony's talk, a bud flowers when he shifts from the global "thangs that happen in the past" to a specific event—"my coat was layin' down in my house"—the high point of a story, the centrally important ingredient for a personal narrative. Moreover, it is worth noting that Anthony corrected without help a number of spoken expressions in inappropriate registers and chose language more appropriate for schoolrooms and written language. When "crep'" becomes "went into," when "crib" becomes "my house," I question how much direct instruction students like Anthony actually need to eliminate inappropriate speech features.

For a teacher, the question becomes the instructional sequence. In a reading class, why instruct in drawing conclusions when a reader cannot pay attention past the first page? Why criticize a new writer's spoken language when the student has just begun to talk, to hear, and to be heard? Whatever instruction might be needed, certainly "word choice" issues are much easier to teach in a revising or editing lesson than during the sensitive moment when Anthony discovers ways to elaborate on a moment of impact, a discourse strategy that is the skeleton of an academic essay.

Year by year and layer by layer research has built an opposition between spoken and written language and has argued that they are distinct from one another. I, too, was saying talk and writing are different from one another, but I was also saying that talk is a prelude to the essays students write. Which is it? As Scholes (1985) had said, dichotomies are untenable.

Had I not read Shirley Brice Heath's (1989b) essay on talk and writing again and again, I might have let that tangle remain. Fortunately, Heath's work pointed a way out. Discussing a line of rhetoricians, starting with Cicero, she reminded me that conversation and essay are interwoven. Historically, the essay had been a continuation of conversations. Essay-writing began as a brief and informal "irregular undigested piece," according to Samuel Johnson, one of the great essayists of the 18th century. At that time, essays appearing in periodicals became a topic for conversation and debate—and so in its very roots, conversation and essay were connected. It is self-evident that things have changed. The essay as usually taught today has been torn away from its conversational roots and is especially out of context for those like Anthony who have no history of Western European tradition. Although essays in schools are now often delegated to gatekeeping roles, the form remains multivoiced and healthy in many periodicals and op-ed pieces—as it has been since its beginning.

However separate talk and writing have become in most academic and social settings today, current emphasis on collaboration returns the multivoiced essay to an earlier time, a time when there was an organic kinship between a certain kind of conversation and a certain kind of writing. And thus beyond the paradox, beyond the either-or, is the kind of interrelatedness I had been looking for.

In Retrospect: What I Learned

My research had given me clear protection against the many distortions that had been used as bludgeons against the students I taught. First, I had disconnected forever the notion that these students' lack of literacy meant a lack of intelligence. Second, I knew that students who had had trouble in school were not necessarily deficient in spoken language but rather unacquainted with cues that signaled academic styles. Finally, I would never again polarize oral and written cultures. In the end, with classroom research beginning to make a place for itself, with more and more publications about classrooms and by teachers, I knew that somehow we classroom teachers had begun, at the very least, to mark a trail, to be part of a growing reciprocity between experience and knowledge and between practice and theory.

Chapter 8

Maybell:
Moving Toward an Academic Identity

Can students labeled by others as "school failures" achieve a new class-room identity and begin to see themselves as successful students?

My teaching went on A.D.—After Dissertation—as it had before, except now what had often been intuitive instruction became more explicit. I could put into words some teaching principles and strategies and thus explain to tutors our goals and techniques more clearly. Yet there had been, and there remained, clusters of students whom my tutors and I had not been able to reach, who had closed themselves off from learning.

My question had always been, "What did learning look like to adults who somehow got left out in earlier schooling?" Most of my work so far had been to find ways to turn the school experience around for them and help them succeed as students. I had put on hold my observations that many students brought to class inappropriate school behaviors—this one's temper tantrum or that one's posture of head to desk.

I had mentally shrugged my shoulders and told myself that they had a right to this kind of resistance, to let them go. But now I was seeing a pattern in the problem, and I was complicit. I had started to think of it with Kelly, when it seemed he resisted new learning in order to maintain his identity, to preserve his voice as "Mr. Bellhop" who controls life in the fast lane. I had seen hints of it in students who just wanted to get by and get out—students who did not want school to affect them in any substantial way.

In Practice

I now cast about for a name to fit the problem. Academic journals were full of articles about identity, resistance, and their relation to language and culture. A painful classroom clash drove me to disentangle these issues and focus on the connection between classroom identity and classroom failure. As always I owe my next project to one student—call her Beth.

She was perhaps 30 years old, and she was about the most in-my-face resistant student I could remember. After the second week of the semester, she announced to the class in truly stentorian tones what she thought. In this program, she then wrote, "You don't learn what you should." She wanted something different; she gave that message aloud and then wrote the following:

Things different like style of words, grammar, how to say word in sentences, in sound, homonyms in different meaning. These are the things I look for in a real English class.

She found weaknesses in all the courses–even the computer class, which she acknowledged might help some people but was too short. Her vigorous, constant disgruntlement started to wear on everyone. She refused a writing tutor to help her individually. She refused whole-group instruction. She had said students "should learn resumes," but when I put together a resume unit, she (predictably, I suppose) already knew how to prepare one. When I suggested she could help others, she said no. She was toughest in a small group, changing the best-humored writing groups into tense or silent exchanges. The semester, mercifully, ended. I would have written those four months off had she not, at the end, written a lengthy response to Langston Hughes's poem "Freedom's Plow":

What this poem means to me is when a man or anyone start with anything they have in their mind, (a dream). Start by clean out youself first. Take out all doubts that you can't do whatever. "You know what to do." Take out all saying like: Oh I can't; Oh I don't know how to start. Oh if I start can I finish; Oh this person said I can't, I guess I won't. So if you can do away with all those doubts in your mind, you can do whatsoever you say and nothing can stand in your way.

After the essay explains how teamwork brings the dream into existence, Beth wrote,

This poem also remember me of Project Bridge, the teachers had a dream . . . and form a union and call it community.

Halfway through, she begins to pick up the cadence the poem offered, writing,

So it wasn't one teacher's dream alone, but all of the Bridge teachers together . . . and when they got the students it became their

world and our world. So that's why Project Bridge belongs to all
that build it.

This last writing suggests that on some level Beth had gotten something from the program and actually had learned a good deal about writing. I could see that but could *she*? Her relentless complaint that not only
I but everyone else did not want her to "get hers" and withheld from her
what she needed to know continued, so much so that an English instructor the next semester asked her dean to get Beth out of her class. She continued vigorously to reject any classroom identity that could have led her
into studenthood.

All at once, as if the "Spirits of Teacher Research" were determined
to show me this issue writ large, I met a veritable briar patch of determined nonrespondents in rapid succession. I saw the football player
called T.C. He was just out of high school, with crew-cut brown hair and
eyes set close together, his head small for his 280-pound frame. He was
late to class every day. When I called him on it, he shrugged a big "So
what?" at me. His first writing was late and empty of content. I met very
briefly Corrina, who on the first day of class walked all the way from
the back of the class to the front, handed me her in-class writing, said
"I don't like writing," and walked out. There was one person who sat
in absolute silence, sometimes with her head on the desk, wrapped in a
hooded sweatshirt.

And there were others. By this point, I could not go on ignoring students who seemed to reject whatever the classroom could offer and refuse
any kind of student identity, students who brought the banner of conflict
to class. Why do they come? What do they want? How do they see themselves in school? I faced, then, one of those crossroads: Down one path
the teacher gets angry and defensive and blames the students. Down the
other the researcher finds in the sometimes uncomfortable classroom new
questions that move beyond one simple answer to a more inclusive vision.
There was no question for me about which path to take.

In Theory: Resistance and Identity

What most influenced my thinking were the many discussions about
resistance and about the development of a classroom identity. Thomas
Newkirk, at the University of New Hampshire, focused on *identity negotiation*. Echoing Erving Goffman's notion of the presentation of self,
Newkirk's *The Performance of Self in Student Writing* (1997) centers on how
identity negotiation occurs. All of us, Newkirk writes,

selectively reveal ourselves in order to match an idealized sense of who we should be. . . . [T]he sense we have of being a "self" is rooted in a sense of competence primarily . . . in social interaction. . . . We feel this competence under attack when our performative routines fail us, in a foreign or hostile setting. (pp. 4–5)

Applying this to the classroom, he asks, finally, what kind of "self" do we invite students to be, and which of students' selves do we "subtly dismiss?"

Robert Brooke, currently teaching at the University of Illinois, began his career at the University of Nebraska, where he shifted instruction from a sequential curriculum to a writing workshop. His role as an instructor changed from being one who taught rhetorical principles to being one who listened and who provided students with "space, time, and encouragement for their own learning" (Brooke, 1991, p. 1). Like other student-centered teachers, Brooke began to put student learning instead of his teaching in the foreground. In this workshop setting, issues of identity became central. In fact, he discovered that the individual's learning to write is secondary to the student's negotiation of a classroom identity: "Writing only becomes meaningful in social interaction, in discussion, thinking and collaboration with others we respect" (1991, p. vii). His book proceeds to describe how this kind of collaborative learning comes about in his classes. For instance, one student, writing from the religious right, had to learn new ways to write about what mattered to him before his new audience found his work persuasive.

One of Brooke's research partners, Joy Ritchie (1989), also wrote about questions of identity—particularly in light of an oft-cited essay by David Bartholomae (1983), who wrote that "[the student] must become like us. . . . He must become someone he is not" (p. 300). Ritchie differs. She takes the stand that writing in the university is not just a single-pronged effort at becoming part of the university; it is also central that the student gain an individual voice within that new setting. She describes two students, Brad and Becky, both of whom seek a voice of their own that will join them to the various cultures surrounding them. Ritchie's point here is that students bring much from their own histories and that they need to integrate that with the new academic culture that surrounds them (Ritchie, 1989, pp. 158–159).

These researchers had, I thought, hit the nail straight: I had spent much time studying how students learned writing, how they engaged with reading, but Project Bridge went beyond reading and writing. We were providing a college in miniature—reading, writing, math, computer literacy, and a content course like biology or sociology—so that students could take a first step into being part of this new academic culture.

It was during the week of orientation that we often first observed how students fit themselves into the roles of studenthood and how each student went about forging a place, a classroom identity. During that week students read and discussed poems in groups, did writing tasks with partners, handed in homework (or did not), and took a reading test. Some students, by hostility or disapproving silence, signaled one kind of message to teachers and peers; others entered into the activities and signaled a different sense of the identity they chose to manifest in the classroom. How did students claim a space in the first days of class? How did this classroom identity change over time? These questions prompted the study that follows.

In Response: The Study

What kind of identities did students declare in their first week of a writing class, and what were their expectations? To answer that question for myself I applied for a National Council of Teachers of English (NCTE) Classroom Inquiry Grant. As both research assistant and tutor, David Mullen agreed to help in class and also to meet privately with each member of a focus group of students. The two of us, armed with various pieces of paper and recording equipment, set out to examine not only expectations but also curriculum and instruction from the student's point of view. When did students engage? Could we begin to understand why those who chose to reject school did so?

Analysis: Questionnaire and Interviews

When school opened in 1992, Project Bridge's 2-day orientation session gave me a chance to give all students in the program, regardless of writing expertise, some open-ended questions about writing that concentrated on three areas: their ideas about good writing, their recollections of earlier school experiences, and their expectations for writing in college. I established three groups of students, based on their answers to this questionnaire.

Group 1. The 25 or so students in the first group knew what they wanted from college and were prepared to achieve it. As in the talk-writing study, the majority of these students had a clear idea of what college writing might entail. Some sought to strengthen their writing as part of their personal growth: "I want to write because I can be happy to say look what I did," one student wrote. Others discussed goals ranging from academic ones ("I need to know how to write for an AA degree") to more personal ones ("I enjoy writing plays and skits"). But under it all rested an interest in achieving what they needed in order to become someone who would move confidently into college-level courses.

These students most likely would have succeeded in many basic writing classes. Given a tutor's help, I anticipated their route into college-level courses would be relatively smooth. And so it proved. One student out of this group, for example, earned an AA degree in 2 years, transferred to the University of California, completed a master's degree, and is now teaching economics at the college. Others were snapped up straight out of school for computer jobs. These are the successful students, and their classroom identity was not, for them or for their teachers, in question.

Group 2. A second group was formed out of eight students who saw themselves literally as returning to elementary school. They sought to repair early schooling, to return to the years when cursive writing was taught—perhaps 4th grade. "I'd like to learn cursif and maybe print better too," one man wrote (in perfectly legible cursive, I might add). This group contained eight students who wanted a new beginning. These students are those who think of writing primarily in terms of the "writing system." Many of them were weaned away from their worry about neatness by introduction to the computers, although several complained in the December follow-up survey that they had not improved in handwriting. Members of this group saw themselves as being in the earliest phase of writing and as working on acquiring our written language system. Acquisition of this level of skill is usually thought of as confined to the first three grades. In actuality, most of the students in this group wrote "cursif" neatly and legibly, but needed to accept that they were much further along in writing development than they thought.

Group 3. The remainder of those entering the class (6 students) responded to the survey in one of two ways. Some answered the questions by saying nothing revealing about themselves. Members of this group responded with "I need to write better to improve my writing" or "I want to improve my reading and math skills." Others said they "hated writing," did not really want to learn how to write, and had never read any writing they cared to mention. Responding to a question about how she learned to write, one student responded, "Use your imagination."

The 14 students from Groups 2 and 3—those who saw themselves as new beginners, those who chose to say nothing and take few risks, and those who declared themselves opposed to learning to write at all— seemed to me most likely to slip through the classroom cracks. Among

them I expected to find the ones least likely to fit into an academic community, to find new roles in classrooms.

Findings from Two Cases

Surveys are notoriously unrevealing, especially in basic skills classes.
To amplify voices too seldom heard—and too often distorted by the written medium through which they are heard—I concentrated on developing portraits of a few students through interviews with the help of David
Mullen, the research assistant who collaborated with me on this project.

The students who were openly hostile to writing refused to join the
project. We chose to profile in detail two "new beginners," willing participants from Group 3 whose responses on the survey also had some answers of the "say nothing revealing" sort.

Kisha. Kisha was a young, slim, well-dressed, and attractive woman—
a firecracker with laughter and anger riding equally near the surface. In
class, a first impression suggested—quite wrongly—a comfortable academic persona.

Her story is perhaps the most classic of all identity struggles. Kisha
grew up in the home of her grandmother. Identified early in grade school
as a special education student, Kisha spent most of her school day in a
pull-out program at "the portables," a program known to her (and hence
to us) as "R.S.P." (Kisha never explained what the acronym R.S.P. meant.)

She laughs with her friends in Project Bridge, but almost never makes
a bid to give an answer. Even in a one-to-one setting, she hesitates on each
response. When David asked her about "what made good writing," she
can only remember her sister's handwriting: "She got lovely handwriting.
It's just wonderful, it's beautiful." A major worry for her, next to her handwriting and spelling, is her speech. In an interview, when David asked her
what would change now that she was learning to write, she said:

> The way I talk. Because I have problems in the way I talk. I have to
> tell you, you can tell . . . I can see you, you can tell by the way I talk
> it's not the full proper English.

When David told her it sounded fine to him, she said, "No. No.
'Cause when I write, I talk the way I . . . when I talk I talk the way I—and
my writin' don't make no sense." She pounded the table as she uttered
the last five words. As David pushed her to explain what was wrong
with her talk, she said, "It's what I say. . . . Yeah, see [laughs] that's what
I mean. It's just how I write and I be 'and,' 'and' I always 'and' 'n 'I will'

you know." After another push to explain why these features are wrong, she said, "Suppose to change it, suppose to change it up a little bit. Even I know that much."

Kisha's recollections about her schooling were not, in general, happy ones. Her grades were always bad. Her sister made A's and B's, but she "got only G's and U's." She felt she missed a great deal. She was taught "how to do math, but we stopped on fractions." In particular, she commented on the lack of writing. She said she had never had a writing class and thus had "no idea" what to expect from our class: "Writing? Well we . . . we wasn't so much on writin all . . . no. They thought we was retarded. . . . They thought we was crazy." She did, however, recognize that she was not exactly like many of these students: She said, "There was some very slower people in there than me."

She knew, up close and personal, why literacy is a key to the adult world. She told David about her firsthand experience needing to read and write. She explained it this way:

> Writing is important because . . . le's see I don't know. It is important because like letters and stuff, docamens, docaments. You have to know how to read 'em and write 'em. It's so important because I had a job with the transit company they wanted me to, ah, read but . . . I wrote good but I just couldn't read that good.

She gave another reason for wanting to write better. She offered the notion that she "oughta write a book. I want the world to know. I'm not ashamed. No I'm not." When David asked her why she wanted to write a book, she told him,

> Because . . . like a life should[n't] be ashamed of. In my life that's what I thought 'cause when I didn't know how to . . . when I didn't know how to read and write I thought it was a shame but it's not a shame for. . . . I need help.

By the time she was in the community college, she no longer needed others to shame her for her language—she did it to herself. About her performance in high school she said,

> See I was a . . . I was a a good student but I just didn't go so I had to go to continuation school. . . . I didn't like coming to school [but] I like to go sit out front. I ain't gon' lie to you. . . . Didn't do nothin', sittin' outside smoking, saying "Sue did what?" and "Sue wore what?" Didn't do NUTHIN. . . . That about it.

The threats to her academic identity were many and varied, but both David and I hoped to interrupt her old pattern of sitting outside. We hoped to bring her in.

Maybell. At the beginning of the semester, Maybell moved into classrooms as if attempting to shrink her 6-foot-tall frame by a foot or two before walking along the walls to a seat. Her eyes were greatly magnified by thick glasses and were hidden when she looked down, and her accent was the drawl of rural Mississippi. In addition, a speech defect caused partly by dental problems upset her so that she rarely spoke. She was at first so withdrawn, so distant from taking her rightful place in the schoolroom, that I held out little hope for her success.

Her interview with David revealed how serious her speech impediment was. The following sample may not do justice to the struggle David faced to understand Maybell's speech—or to the embarrassment of Maybell as she tried to make herself understood:

DAVID: Smokey and I, we'd really like to have a little more information about your writing questionnaire. OK?
MAYBELL: [no response]
DAVID: Here's the first question [reading from the questionnaire]: I want to write because . . .
MAYBELL: [Reading from her answer, as if pronouncing words in a list] I . . . need . . . to . . . learn . . . how . . . to . . . write.
DAVID: Why?
MAYBELL: I wanna get—I wanna, I wanna, get my . . . WORDS. I wanna, you know, uh, see, I'm NERvous and my words don't come out like I . . . WANT them to and you know I don't know how to . . . some I know how to write some words I could put down on paper what I think in my MIND, and . . .
DAVID: You want to get the ideas out of your head and down on paper?
MAYBELL: On paper, uh huh.

She was extremely sensitive about making others understand her—in talk or writing. She told David, "See I'm tie-tongued. People ask me four or five time 'what did I say?' I say, I be talkin it again but it come out the same way. . . ." Behind this concern was another layer of worry about speaking proper English. But this insecurity about speaking African American English was almost never mentioned in spite of multiple prompts in interviews and in class.

As I transcribed her interview, I wondered again and again how best to help Maybell become less strained and more comfortable in school. I noticed her tangled sentences and her all-but-inaudible voice. If speech was difficult and writing was even harder, I did not have answers. But I did not know her determination. When David asked her what kinds of writing she knew about besides job applications and insurance papers, she reads again from her questionnaire response:

> MAYBELL: I . . . know . . . people . . . that . . . have . . . nice . . . hand-writin'. . . . My sister Emma have nice handwritin' and you know [student name] he have nice handwritin'.
> DAVID: What's nice about it?
> MAYBELL: You know it be nice like they want it all the same. If they can—If I can do it—nah, if they can do it I can do it.

Her early school experience in rural Mississippi was apparently a pleasant time, a time when she and her brothers and sisters (10 of them I believe she said) walked home together. She did not attend regularly and seems to have stopped school during the 4th or 5th grade, but her attitude toward that experience seems mostly positive. She spoke of her favorite teacher, "Mrs. Wright," who "help me to write, and pronounce my words." And she had memories of comma instruction. It seemed that as instruction became harder, she left school, though we can only infer a connection between difficulty and school leaving. Her last word on what she remembered about first learning to write is linked with her withdrawal from class:

> She [Mrs. Wright] tried, she tried to, you know, get the periods in the right place, but I didn't. I was doin it but I had some trouble in the family. My parents got sick and I just couldn't do it no more, I couldn't do my homework.

She did not see her withdrawal from school as a decision she should not have made: It did not sound like a decision she made at all. She did not feel like school had failed her (or that she had failed school).

The Project Bridge class she was enrolled in was difficult for her because it conflicted with her idea that handwriting should be neat. She said, "It's a ways Smokey want it . . . but you know I'm not able to sit down and write like other people. . . . I try not to go down a hill with it. That's the way I was raised."

By midterm, however, she said in her interview that she could see improvement because "I used to write all down a hill." There were other important changes that took place. Although she was still concerned because she wrote slowly, she also wrote more fully and fluently. With her successes in writing, her sense of self-esteem began to bloom. In her final interview, she said,

> Once I used to just be at home, doin nuthin eating everything I could get my hands on, getting bigger than the house, but now I feel good inside. Then I used to be depressed. I needed to write more because my writing is working good I see myself as writing better than I did when I first came.

And what was the turning point? There may have been several, two of which I have captured here. First, just as Maybell had promised, her speech and her writing improved together. She said,

> At first I was scared. I didn't talk to nobody my questioning and Smokey she was there. The others they'd be laughing. I don't like people laughing. I didn't raise my hand or answer. I can do it now. I ain't scared of it. I can say "shut up okay and let me talk, okay, you all talk all semester an now it's my turn."

Second, her participation in writing groups was critical to her sucess. At first, she said,

> [I] didn't want nobody to touch it [her paper]. But Smokey said get in a group and we get in a group and we do a lot of things. . . . She had us feel each other's skin and stuff and write is it soft? Does it stink? Is it fresh? That's what she had us do and, shoot, I enjoyed Bridge.

At the end of the semester, she wrote an essay about her sister. It's hard not to notice a new freedom and authority in her writing:

My Sister Mazell

My sister Mazell is strong. She's not very tall but she has powerful arms and lighter skin than I do. Mazell had this friend by the name of Jerry Bush. He used to come over to the house. While they were playing cards, he would come in and say, "Mazell, get me a glass of water." Mazell would say, "You know where the kitchen's at." My sister told Jerry Bush to leave her the hell alone, but he couldn't . . .

Jerry Bush know how Mazell got when someone was bothering her, but he didn't know how strong Mazell really was until she picked him up and threw him out of the stone glass door. I bet he found out when she picked his butt up and he went flying out that door. It happened back at our family home in Mississippi. When I came in the door, Jerry was going out like a jet. Our neighbor called the police. They did not send one car. They sent three cars out to see what was going on in [our family] home. Some of the policemen knew us well because that is how it is in Mississippi; the police know everybody. . . . The police came and they took him to the hospital. All this happened a couple months after my mother's death. Smokey, Mazell was pregnant at the time when she did what she did to Mr. B. The baby came alright but she isn't a baby any more. She's bigger than her mother Mazell. But what I remember about those two is Jerry Bush flying out the door, and Mazell three months pregnant.

The Two Cases: Making Meaning

Maybell developed a positive classroom identity, and several of the means by which she developed her abilities were strategies she worked out independently. Kisha, after a lifetime on the outside of success, failed in this endeavor. What can we learn from these two students who seem so different–one so promising who was not successful, one so unpromising who succeeded?

These two women, Kisha and Maybell, were each at highest risk for school failure. They both gave similar reasons for their precarious grip on school, reasons which each perceived to be her personal fault. Each blamed herself for her lack of neatness, her inability to write a smooth, even cursive, and for not having "good writing."

Further, both students shared a conviction that their use of African American Vernacular English was the root of their problems with writing. Their concern—sometimes spoken about, sometimes revealed nonverbally—was to speak and write the "full proper English," a language they did not claim for their own. In addition, they both carried with them rules, such as forbidding the use of "I" and writing on the line and not "down-a-hill."

And yet as the semester went along, Kisha changed from the "good student" we'd seen during the first days of class. Maybell, who had seemed hopelessly lost at first, developed an active and successful academic place as the semester progressed. Their grades tell what happened, though they say nothing about why the one remained on the margins and the other jumped into the middle. Maybell received an A with three units of credit: Its significance is that she attended each class for a total of at least 45 hours over the semester. She had almost perfect attendance; a full, reflective journal; and several finished essays. Kisha received a below-passing grade for a single unit, since, in all, she had scarcely attended more than 15 times; she had no completed writings by the semester's end.

What turned out to be of greater weight than the features they shared were their differences, particularly their differences in self-perception. Kisha grew up in an urban family and always felt herself to be neglected by her mother and overshadowed by her siblings. Labeled as learning disabled when she was young, she had been given many opportunities to develop skills, but she continued to see herself as a "retard" and to fight that stigma. Maybell was part of a strong rural family. She did not have a lot of formal education in the Mississippi classroom and was given almost no special attention. She never did learn, for example, when to use *two* or *to* and *know* or *no*. She may have had her own eye-ear-hand disconnection that could be called a learning disability, but it had never been identified.

Kisha remained obsessed with whether or not her earlier school experience marked her as lacking intelligence. In a poignant free writing she said, "I know I was one of them students that was not so hot in class. . . . But now I look back and know I am not really crazy I'm a human just like the real brightest student." But she could never seem to locate a topic to write about. Maybell, on the other hand, just charged ahead, trying everything. She earned her place as a student in part because she behaved like a student. She spent a great deal of time at home trying different kinds of writing. She used two strategies with great effectiveness: The first was the use of literature as a model for her writing, and the second was the use of African American rhetorical devices.

For Maybell, there remained many gaps. She found it difficult to explain concepts such as "the writing process," at least in the later part of the second month of class. Her final essay about her sister was the work of several weeks, and no doubt tutors eliminated what they perceived to be egregious errors. But that does not dim the progress she did make toward declaring herself a student. In light of her early fear of entering the classroom, it is a remarkable achievement. Kisha never reached that threshold.

In Retrospect: "If They Can Do It, I Can Do It"

These two students suggest how belief in oneself and acceptance of one's possibilities—and of one's own language—are woven together to promote a comfortable academic identity. Kisha's view of herself as "crazy" or "retarded" conflicts with all efforts to persuade her otherwise. At every word of encouragement, Kisha looks with condescension at the speakers, as if she knows better. Her conviction that she cannot do it trumps all the cards outsiders offer her with their "I know you can," or "Just don't give up." She wins the argument but loses the game. Kisha believed that others in her neighborhood or in her college class were laughing at her. She suspected the reason was her long-ago R.S.P. school placement. However farfetched that may seem, she believed it wholeheartedly.

Fifteen years ago Shirley Brice Heath (1989a) suggested that literacy is part of a community effort in Southern enclaves, with everyone contributing to the making of meaning, while in urban settings young African Americans may well be left essentially on their own. This could be at heart responsible for why Kisha—definitely alone in her daily activities—felt unsupported. Our program gave Kisha the best shot we could, but it was clearly insufficient. Perhaps she (and many others like her) cannot overcome the label of "special student" and cannot overcome the early shame. Both David and I always hoped that she would stop sitting outside; again and again we invited her to the room, but she never could take that step over the threshold.

But then there are students like Maybell who accepted the invitation. It is students like Maybell (and Rose and Anthony and Ruth and so many others) who show us that it is not necessary to hold adult learners' hands all the way to adult academic development. It is only necessary to bring them into their own engagement with learning. At that point, their intelligence will lead them the rest of the way.

Part V

WRITING IT UP

One of the dominant themes in this book is the importance of teachers' sharing their work. They need to share not only their questions, focus, data, and analysis, but also their ideas, their discussion. What do the findings mean? The final chapter in this volume is devoted to that task.

As the "Guide" emphasizes, teachers need to reach out to other teachers and speak about what they have learned and what they do not yet know. Teacher research can serve various purposes: It can improve the teachers' classrooms, and it can affect entire schools, administrations, and school boards. It can send information about local settings to the radar screens of state and federal governments so that they will be better informed. Accordingly, teachers are usually spoken of as "action researchers."

But equally important, in my view, is that without the work of teacher-researchers, the research university would be unable to give teachers answers to the many questions that haunt us.

Chapter 9

—

Reflections:
Lessons from Classroom Research

What can a teacher's reflections tell us that we cannot learn any other way?

Many urban communities appear to outsiders to be desolate wastelands, empty of shops or restaurants, full of deserted streets and as dangerous as the Badlands of a Hollywood Western after dark. I know the community I met in 1965 struck me with just such a sense of desolation. It took several years to gain a more accurate impression of the neighborhoods I saw every day. Within those homes, newborns come home from hospitals, go to schools, marry, and have children of their own, often settling near the houses or streets where they grew up. Not until I had begun teaching the children, nieces, best friends—and even the children's children—of former students did I understand the overriding values of the stalwarts in these spaces: family, education, religion.

THE STUDENTS I CAME TO KNOW

Above all, in this community many—and especially the older generations—hold education in esteem. Even though they didn't have much faith in their own or their teachers' abilities to repair schooling broken in grade school or high school, they still come to college (or send their children) seeking higher education.

All over America, there are families and communities about whose literacy and schooling we know little. Some of these communities lie within the larger city, like the ones I have come to know. Others are rural. Most of their families speak a nonstandard variety of English. We speak often of literacy as a global issue and look to other nations for implications for instruction at home. Researchers and policy makers encourage work from "beyond our own borders," as we read in the American Educational Research Association (AERA) 2007 convention theme statement, titled "The

World of Educational Quality." And yet there are also worlds within our own national borders that we do not know, students for whom educational quality is a sometimes thing. We can look beyond what we know, not necessarily by going to a new place, but by looking at what we see every day with new eyes.

Theory Into Practice: Regarding School Success

From my studies, I not only have found teaching strategies for classrooms but also have gained insight into the act of shaping writing from talk. As all those voices I had heard over the years played back in my mind—Gloria, Ruth, Maybell, Mark, Anthony, Kelly—I gained a panoramic view of answers to questions I had at last learned to put into words: What kinds of interactions help learners convert the talk they are most comfortable with—often nonstandard talk—into the written language that schools demand, a written form that feels to them at first stiff and foreign?

But issues from beyond the classroom have waited for a hearing. It is important that we shine light on macrosocial issues. I return to questions I began with so long ago in the college's Reading Lab: Why are so many African American adults—competent in so many aspects of their lives—still finding themselves "strangers in academia," as Mina Shaughnessy (1977) noticed so long ago? This situation has changed little in 30 years. What is it we are not seeing?

In Classrooms: Transforming Talk Into Writing

My work has been guided by Lev Vygotsky's idea that learning is based in the social order, that a something intervenes between minds and raw experiences. The wherewithal that aids the development of higher mental functions are tools that, via social interaction, mediate between the known and the not-yet-grasped. This first intervention is interpsychological—used between people, for example between a parent and child or a teacher and student.

After the task is learned, what had been external becomes internal, or intrapsychological. The mediation then becomes an internal cognitive process—we can talk ourselves through deciphering an unknown word or solving a fractions problem. The examples that follow are those I have researched in libraries and tried in my teaching practice. I have described only a part of it in this volume. Throughout, my work owes much to Vygotsky's idea of the zone of proximal development and concentrates on identifying strategies whereby the tutor mediates and collaborates with inexperienced writers to shift from spoken language to literate practices.

Strategy 1: Scaffolding Essays

One of the best known strategies is *scaffolding*, or guided question-response. Since teacher questions and student responses are a part of most teachers' practice, we take such classroom talk for granted. Through observing the following interaction between Awele (tutor) and Cara (student), we can see an example of the interpsychological at work as the tutor's conversation helps shape the student's talk for writing. Awele is an African American woman and an accomplished actress and storyteller who served as a tutor in basic writing classes over several years. Cara is also an African American woman and is in her late twenties. She had been an office worker before wholesale layoffs and had lived on both East and West Coasts. So while extended interaction with Awele might not have been critical for Cara's academic survival, it was needed for her academic growth and writing progress.

Awele's carefully crafted questions led Cara to say what she would later write down. If left on her own to tell about "a learning experience" (the suggested subject for this essay), Cara might have thought of a learning experience on her own and told it well enough. However, the tutor's questions helped the student write a lively essay rather than a ho-hum essay. As shown by the sample of the tutor's talk, Cara's responses, and portions drawn from Cara's writing, Cara and Awele collaboratively developed the written work. The dialog and the extract from the essay presented here show the movement from talk to writing. The dialog shows the back-and-forth collaboration the two share:

> AWELE: Do you have a day in mind? Can you remember back on an experience that was very important? That you can remember? The details? What happened?
>
> CARA: I guess I can remember what happened when I first started to learn how to drive.
>
> AWELE: OK, how old were you at that time?
>
> CARA: Fifte::en
>
> AWELE: OK, can you remember the day that . . . you first . . . sat behind the wheel?
>
> CARA: I think it was, uh, 1968? Or '69?
>
> AWELE: And what kind of a car were you in?
>
> CARA: A '68, ummm, Impala? [doubtful]
>
> AWELE: An Impala, brand new? What color was it? Can you remember?
>
> CARA: Green . . . lime green.

AWELE: Lime green. And how many doors? Was it a two door, four
     door?
CARA: Four door.
Awele: And was anyone with you at the time?
CARA: My stepfather.

The talk continues as the pair works out an entire essay. What is notable is the way that the tutor's emphasis on detail—"lime green"—shapes
the language the student transfers to the page:

> One morning in July of 1968 A thought came to mind What it was
> like behind the wheel of a car
>   I was about 15 years old at the time I got into our 1968 Impaya. It
> was big with four door and painted lime green in side and out.
>   I make sure the car was in park. I looked over my left shoulder
> I got the car away from the carb I looked in the rear view mirror to
> see a car coming over my Left shoulder I hit the brakes, me and my
> father almost went through the front window.

From the tutor's questions, we can almost extract the rubric by which
the first essay will be evaluated. The tutor, of course, knows the critical
elements of this kind of narrative-descriptive essay. She offers a set of directions in her first comments:

> *A specific experience*: "Do you have a day in mind?"
> *A memory*: "Can you remember back on an experience?"
> *A highly engaging event*: "Can you remember back on an experience
>   that was very important?"
> *An event with sensory recollections*: "[Can you remember] The details?"
> *A chronological event*: "[Can you remember] What happened?"

The student locates an appropriate topic immediately. The tutor ac-
cepts it, perhaps because it has been cast into a narrative frame: a specific
memory of a learning experience common to American adolescents.
     After the tutor's questions lay out the details of the background—
when, *where*, and *who*—she asks for action: "What happened?" The student
begins at the beginning of the event, as the tutor implies she should: "First
he told me . . . then he say . . ." As the action unfolds, the tutor hints that
the tale needs a moment of intensity, a moment when the emotions shape a
high point in the narrative. In a part of the narrative I've not included, the
tutor asks, "You're in the middle of the road, what happened then?" The
student complies with dramatizing a near-wreck: "I almost went through
the windshield." The two continue in this way for 35 speech turns until
the student's story and its significance are laid out.

We may take such an achievement for granted, but it is not easy to start up a conversation in which one asks the questions and the other provides information about her life. Yet when it works, the essay is richer than it might have been without the conversation. This question-answer strategy is the meat-and-drink of classrooms. While primary-grade teachers are expected to assist youngsters to form stories, as Sarah Michaels (1986) pointed out in her description of 1st-grade sharing time, we rarely imagine it may be needed with adults. Yet such assistance is indispensable when teachers want to show an adequate writer the road to becoming a better writer.

Strategy 2: Scaffolding Words and Sentences

This strategy is also helpful with less sophisticated writers. Ruth, the student featured in Chapter 6, was a very new writer. Nevertheless, the opening comments between the tutor and Ruth practically replicate Awele and Cara's beginning. In both, the tutor repeats words that are central to the writing task ("an *incident* that sticks out," "an *incident* you'd like to write about").

Scaffolding remains the basic structure of Ruth and her tutor's interaction, and it proceeds smoothly toward the development of a narrative. Because tutors control the conversation in scaffolded exchanges, it is often a preferred style. Once learners begin to talk spontaneously, however, the task is more challenging, especially with those whose spoken language is far from standard and who are not yet adequate writers.

In extended exchanges, teachers intuitively, almost below the threshold of awareness, shape talk into writing. How do tutors and teachers "learn" to do this? I do not argue that we "teach" written language explicitly. Rather, our tacit expectations that information should be presented in accord with written conventions tends to stay below the surface, below the level of our conscious linguistic awareness. Ruth's tutor shows that teaching is art as well as science. In her interaction with Ruth, the tutor intuitively made use of four original, improvised strategies (listed below). Each is subtle and easily overlooked, yet each shapes spoken language into written forms.

1. Putting nonverbal information into words
2. Restatement: Providing standard English pronunciation
3. Adjusting and repairing talk for writing
4. Reordering information

1. Putting Nonverbal Information Into Words. Earlier chapters have stressed the ways gestures, mime, acting out parts, and other nonverbal devices contribute to the colorful styles of some speakers. These devices, however, must shift in written form. The following interaction between the tutor and Ruth shows how the descriptive detail the tutor wants the student to use, the taste of an herbal concoction, can be put into words:

> RUTH: It tasted like when they grind your teeth. [Rubs teeth back and forth]
> TUTOR: Powdery?
> RUTH: Yeah like a powder.

2. Restatement: Providing Standard English Pronunciation. In another example of the tutor's help in finding words useful in elaborating the taste of this herbal treatment, the tutor restates the student's word:

> RUTH: It had a urka-surka feeling.
> TUTOR: Like Alka-Seltzer, like bubbles . . .

Ruth and her tutor intertwine their language to develop the story of the father's herbal treatment of the child's lowland fever. The translation of "urka-surka" into "Alka-Seltzer" is one of those brilliant interactive moments when the conversational ball has been tossed high and wide, and the teacher (it seems effortlessly) catches the word, reshapes it, and tosses it back to the student—that is, she ignores what she physically hears and catches the student's intended meaning of the "urka-surka" feeling that eases a stomachache. We take this kind of tutor–student understanding as natural and inevitable. It is neither. It would be easy to overlook Ruth's point completely, say "huh?" or laugh or respond without understanding. I remember, with a twinge, just such blunders when I drilled Mark about words I did not understand.

3. Adjusting and Repairing Talk for Writing. The following interaction adjusts talk in preparation for writing and operates at the word or sentence level. It also lays the groundwork for cohesion in a longer piece. For example, a major student error is pronoun reference. It goes without saying that written language demands a link, a referent, between a pronoun and the "last-mentioned noun," but talk permits a less strict relation between noun and pronoun. The example below clarifies the talk and helps the student shift into written mode:

> TUTOR: Can you think of any other stories about friends and family you'd like to write about? Would you like to tell more about him?
> RUTH: I know he was uh ole Creek Indian. He like to go around in the woods and gather these herbs?
> TUTOR: Who, your father?
> RUTH: My father, 'n he like to make his own medicines.

At the end of this exchange pronoun reference is made explicit with the repetition of "father" and the emphasis on "he" and "him."

Even when tutor and student are already in sync, the conversational thread can get tangled. In the example below, it is only when the student spells the word ("a C-O-W") that tutor and student suddenly understand each other. The spoken and written varieties become intertwined. Here, the student is describing her father's ingredients in the recipe for an herbal remedy to cure fever:

> RUTH: After the time, uh, deceased, uh, a, a cow deceased a cow in the woods he would go out 'n get the <u>horns</u> from the cow body . . . a <u>cow</u> . . .
>
> TUTOR: A car?
>
> RUTH: You know like a cah, a C-O-W, a cow.
>
> TUTOR: Ohh, ohh, okay.

Speakers of the Southern regional dialects—particularly those strongly influenced by the Gullah-based African American dialect used on the Gulf Coast—often pronounce *ow* less like the *ou* in *ouch* and more like the sound of *au* in *caw*. The southern dialect also frequently drops the sound of a final *r*, hence the tutor's guess ("A car?") is plausible. Through Standard English orthography ("a c-o-w") the student at last makes her speech understandable to the tutor.

4. Reordering Information. Perhaps the most subtle technique I observed is the way a tutor rearranges the placement of information. The following exchange moves information to the front of the narrative where it provides background, and foregrounds Ruth's "ro-matic fever" by placing it last in the more prominent position:

> TUTOR: Were you ever sick? And did he use [herbs] on you?
>
> RUTH: Yes I was once. I had this fever. I don't know what kind of fever it was but it happen to me when I was seven years old.
>
> TUTOR: Why don't you just TELL me about that?
>
> RUTH: When I was seven years old, I fell sick with a fever and it was the kind of fever they uh call a ro-matic fever.

At first, the movement of this detail seems to be unimportant. But reflection points to a subtle but significant reshaping. It more closely matches William Labov's narrative model (1972b, p. 370): orientation (*who, when, where*), complicating action or event, and evaluation (or *coda*). In her first statement, Ruth places the least important information last ("but it happen to me when I was seven years old"). And after the tutor's request to repeat ("just TELL me about that"), Ruth subordinates her age ("When I was seven") to the more important complicating action ("I fell sick with a fever"). Ruth does not provide new information; she simply reshapes what she has said to fit the conventions of writing.

Ruth, like others I have worked with, did not need one-on-one guidance forever. Once students are able to overcome a few major obstacles, they begin to devise their own particular and sometimes peculiar strategies for writing. Kisha and Maybell, the students in Chapter 8, illustrate the watershed difference between the two: Kisha did not develop independent writing strategies, and Maybell did.

Maybell's three interviews with David spanned the semester and provide valuable insights into one instance of a developing academic identity. We were fortunate to capture her testimony regarding how she took in information and how she went from silence to speaking up. Early in the semester, she said often how frightened she was of other people. At grocery stores she shopped early in the morning so she would not see anyone. In class she did not want anyone touching her or her paper. Not only did she fear our invasion of "her space," but she also dreaded our reaction to her talk—and she was, in a way, right, for we could not understand what she said. During this period, her shyness or anxiety was high. Concepts delivered in lecture were difficult for her to take in. She complained about noise from others, but the problem was deeper than a talkative seatmate. Nevertheless, as Chapter 8 describes, her self-confidence and competence slowly grew.

The measure of Maybell's beginning academic success is her ability to absorb a large-group "minilecture," albeit a lecture of only 5 minutes. After this, David and I observed an increase in her ability to learn as part of a group, and to let go of the need for one-on-one attention. I had devised minilectures in order to discover if or when students like Maybell begin to absorb and function within whole group instruction. I gave two minilectures that semester, one at the beginning of the semester, one after 6 weeks.

To Maybell, the first minilecture was just so many minutes of white noise. During the interview with David right after, Maybell reviewed the 5-minute videotape from class in which I listed some steps or stages writers go through. I called it the "writing process," and explained it by drawing an analogy to space travel. One would not just jump off into space without preparation; one first needs to build a spaceship, complete special training, try practice runs, and so on. In the same way, I said, good writing needs preparation: brainstorming ideas, free writing, drafting, and letting others hear it. David stopped the VCR at the end of this vignette and asked Maybell to explain the writing process as she understood it. She said that she never *had* understood really what it was. She misinterpreted the point of this minilecture and recast the message as a personal one: "Smokey was telling me to go for it, [that I could get] whatever I wanted if I'd try."

By midterm, when David and Maybell started the second interview, they viewed another brief videotaped minilecture. It was clear that after 6 weeks she was learning in a whole-group setting. The lesson I had emphasized was the need for focus: to select a single action or event when writing a narrative. I emphasized that "putting five different chapters of your life story on one page" would leave all the topics underdeveloped. This time Maybell understood. When David asked her what that lesson was about, she replied:

> Our impact paper, that's what she's talking about. 'Cause we had to write a impact paper about one thing. Some people had two or twelve chapters all on one page like me, I didn't know how many I had I was writing about my momma and my daddy and my sister 'n all . . .

As I learned by studying Maybell's daily "reflective journal" closely, her writing strengthens from the first entry, a 6- to 8-line piece about "A Labor Day Picnic," to a midpoint in the semester. For the first 6 weeks, or into mid-October, she copied verbatim many writings: a well-known poem about "Mr. Cocaine," short articles from newspapers on "Wildfire," "Drugs," "Nuclear Threat," poems to Mother, and so on. From this practice she began to absorb the sentence structures and flow of writing. The transition from word-by-word copying to personal subjects moved through what she called "summary." I started every writing class by handing out and reading aloud a short, imagistic piece, say by Mark Twain or Langston Hughes. The instructions said, "Listen to the reading as long as you want, but if any sentence or image triggers a writing idea, start writing."

By November, Maybell no longer copied passages word for word. Instead, she adopted the published author's sentence structure, and intertwined her own words with his. For example, Langston Hughes's short story "Salvation" describes his being "saved from sin" at a revival. The point of his narrative is that he went through with the baptism but he was both sad and enraged that Jesus had not appeared to him. Maybell missed that point, but her "Summary of Langston Hughes" showed her integrating the author's graceful sentence structures with her own.

Here is one sentence from "Salvation": "Then I was left all alone on the mourners' bench. My aunt came and knelt . . . the whole congregation was praying just for me." Here is Maybell's version: "Langston did not want to be the only one left on the mourners' bench. His aunt was on her knees crying and praying and singing. The congregation was singing for him alone." She uses Hughes's language as a template, placing her own words in the framework his prose offers. It is clear, though, that she brings to this writing her own experiences with revivals and mourner's benches.

A second technique, perhaps based on readings from writers like Langston Hughes, was an independently developed use of African American rhetorical devices. Most striking was the unique voice she developed, as "My Sister Mazell" in Chapter 8 shows. In that piece, she reveals a robust, proud, and vigorous "that's who we are" style. Through "My Sister Mazell," we hear the culture spoken by (and speaking through) the individual. And now that writing has become more familiar to Maybell, we can also hear her relax into her language in its written form as she draws on stylistic features from African American discourse.

In *Talkin' and Testifyin'*, Geneva Smitherman (1977) introduced features of African American discourse into the parlance of the academic community. These "devices of indirection" (termed *signifying* in African American discourse) overlap with some classical features of Western rhetoric (Smitherman, quoted by Carol Lee, 2000, pp. 198–199). These features include exaggerated language, mimicry, proverbs and aphorisms, word play, image making, boasting, loud talking, and lyrical effects (including repetition, alliteration, and special effects such as lengthened vowels and unusual placement of accent).

Maybell primarily uses mimicry, direct address, imagery, and rhythmic sentences that echo the spoken language of those whose lives she shares with us. In "My Sister Mazell," she often mimics the voices of her sister's boyfriend—"Hey Mazell get me a glass of water"—as well as her sister—"You know where the kitchen is." She also uses direct address ("Smokey, Mazell was pregnant . . .").

Her imagery picks up the rhythm of colloquial speech: "She picked his butt up and he went flying out that door." She uses parallel structure for contrast to good effect: "When I came in that door, Jerry was going out like a jet." We could multiply these examples from that piece alone, but the point is that after a semester of practice she is making her own kind of writing useful in school.

IN THEORY: A REVIEW OF SOCIAL CONSTRUCTION

Are these innovative discoveries merely serendipitous accidents, coming as they do from students like Maybell who seem poorly equipped to contribute so much to our understanding of the shifts from spoken to written language? Seen in the light of socially constructed practices, theory has named these linguistic and cognitive developments as more than mere flukes.

The notion that we learn through collaboration with others is more or less in the public domain these days, sole property of no one and yet refined and elaborated upon by many researchers. In its broadest terms, social contructivism is "a theory about knowledge and learning that describes what knowing is and how one comes to know" (Ball, 2000, p. 230). This notion is usually recognized as being rooted in Vygotsky's notions of the ways culture and language influence human development, but also in Michael Bakhtin's notions about meaning making and language use (see Ball, 2000, p. 232). And it has influenced the thought of most major thinkers from 1972 (see Gumperz & Herashimchuk's [1972] discussion of a child-directed collaborative tutoring session) to the present day (see Ball's [2000] discussion of the essential role interaction plays in promoting teacher change). Certainly the various facets of this theoretical concept have influenced me by clarifying how classroom interactions have promoted (or retarded) school success.

Initially Maybell seemed able to "learn" only from one-on-one instruction. As the semester progressed, she could take in ideas presented in whole-group settings. She had begun to let in ideas from the outside world and she began to interact closely with her small group. By the end of the semester she was advising others in class that it was "her turn" to talk. What happened to Maybell in the courses she took that semester? I cannot know for certain that anything happened, but I believe it did, and I think I have seen similar trajectories of growth in others over the years. I found the beginnings of this understanding as I read and reread Vygotsky's writings on thinking. I returned again and again to his idea of two realms, the public and the private. The private space, he proposed, contains all of our implicit knowledge: our intuitions, our taken-for-granted sense or mother-wit, our condensed and personal images or words. In the other realm, the public domain, the highly contextualized personal, becomes the abstract generalization. The sensory impression becomes the detailed subject and predicate: The sense of pleasure when looking at the ocean becomes "I stood transfixed by the startling white sails against the blue of the sky and water." It almost goes without saying that school is the locale of detailed subject and predicate, the locale of lists, categories, and explicit language, and that the conflict between that domain and the personal and private is the barrier that Maybell overcame (Wertsch, 2000, pp. 22–23). Perhaps what happened for her was a new ability to move from one domain to the other, from the personal to the public.

Maybell's gradually increasing ability to move between these domains made concrete for me Vygotsky's ideas about learning. I have already talked about how he held that learning first takes place among people (interpsychological) but eventually takes place within the individual (intrapsychological). This is the route toward learning taken by many of the students described in this book.

Further, these concepts clarified for me certain teaching errors. For example, my efforts to describe "sequence" in reading before students even had books in their hands led to a response like, "['sequence,' are] shiny things I had on my prom dress." My instruction was inevitably unsuccessful: I had not prepared the class for a deductive process ("Here's the idea, and now you'll see an example of it"). More successful was my colleague who waits until the student writes a run-on sentence before teaching end-stop punctuation.

Vygotsky's notion of the explicit versus the implicit, of the deductive procedures of school versus the inductive procedures of daily life, has the power to relate and clarify experiences no matter how distant and distinct they may be. In my own work, I have scarcely done more than identify one or two constellations against a space filled with unknown bodies. Much more waits to be understood. We must walk carefully here, however. Public and private carry the threat of yet another "killer dichotomy," and remind us to be alert for that which reconciles the opposites. The great mediator, the "tool of tools," may be language itself, that which enables us to travel back and forth between the inner and outer worlds. It is language that transports us through the zone of proximal development, that space in which, as Carol Lee and Peter Smagorinsky (2000) put it, teaching can extend the student beyond what he or she could do alone, but without breaking the links to what the learner already knows.

In Response: What We Can Learn from Classroom Research

In studying adults who have long ago passed the so-called critical period of language development, I was at first stymied by the kinds of rapid learning I saw around me. What happened to that critical period, the window from ages 4 to 7? Vygotsky's view of learning—that capacity is not "topped off," not limited or bounded—put my mind at ease. I believe others speaking of lifelong learning agree with this notion. While we once thought language learning ended early, we now know that learning can take place at many points over the span of a lifetime.

In their introduction to a collection of modern works based on Vygotsky's thought, Lee and Smagorinsky (2000) discuss the notion of capacity in this way: Learning *can* take place at any age. Whether or not it *will* take place depends on what the learner already knows, what task is to be learned, what activity structures are present for learning to take place, and what the quality of the person's interactions with others is (p. 2). In other words, as many researchers have shown and Lee and Smagorinsky emphasize, context and capacity are "intricately intertwined."

Several chapters in their volume emphasize how "activity structures" such as writing-conference pairs can help students produce written language. But here is the catch: Interactions may be keys to the doors that open boundless learning, but not just any old interaction will do. It must be of a certain kind: smooth, with repairs of misunderstandings taking the edge off rough spots.

Throughout this volume I have focused on what goes on in the classroom and the importance of teacher research. But there are huge societal issues that go beyond the classroom that need to be recognized. The ghosts of Mark, Kelly, Kisha, and so many others remain part of an invisible crowd that passes through schooling untouched. What happened to them? What left them on the wrong page for so long? Was it one thing, or were there many different issues?

Two students illustrate the complex causes that bring about school difficulties. In both cases, their early years show us what magic we expect from our teachers and how little credit teachers receive when they do help a youngster in high school or junior high to turn a life around. Wanting to understand Darleen in Chapter 6, who never really learned to read, I asked her to share with me a copy of her grade school cumulative folder (i.e., her teachers' comments collected yearly during elementary school) and her high school transcripts. In the section for teachers' comments, from 1958 (when she was 7) to 1962, the school repeatedly recommended eyeglasses. In 1964, the mother made an appointment with an optometrist, but by the end of that year Darleen still had no vision correction. Similarly, from the first year, the nurse's comments began reporting problems: anemic, "mouth-breather." Both dental and medical appointments were recommended yearly, but the years passed. By 1968, according to these records, neither had been taken care of although (again according to the nurse) she had many abscessed teeth. The school alerted the family, but it seemed no one could follow through—not school, not family, not community.

Darleen's teachers' comments, too, hint at problems. She was present only 40 days in the first year, only 15 the second. By Grade 2, one teacher commented she was "slow." Thereafter, each teacher offered a variation on these labels: "very slow," "immature," "poor writing," "short attention span." The repetitiveness of the curriculum would not have inspired attention: She was in a K–1 class for three semesters. The first year, she studied caterpillars, gold fish, and (it appears from the blurred copy I have) beavers. The next semester, ditto—plants, animals, and trains. In addition, number readiness was introduced. The next semester, more of the same—birds, fish, and snails; reading readiness was introduced. She was in pre-primers in 1st grade. Not until 1960, when she was 9 years old, did the school offer the primers 1, 2, and 3—*Fun with Dick and Jane.*

Her 1st-grade teacher offered the first compliment recorded in the "special abilities" column. She said she "tries hard." Other teachers concurred: "likes to learn," is "enthusiastic," "helpful." It began to look as though each teacher copied the comments of the previous year. Her academic progress was not mentioned. When she was 13, tests for special education identified a low IQ and (based on the Gray oral) a reading level "adequate at 2nd grade." When she came to community college 30 years later, her reading test had not changed much.

In short, the school offered little academic stimulation, and she came to school with health problems that no doubt made learning difficult if not impossible. She could not see the blackboard through much of her elementary school. She started school with problems that predated the classroom and that continued for a number of years. Against those odds, I wonder what a lone teacher with 30 other youngsters could have done.

Darleen may have had problems with seat work and with *Fun with Dick and Jane*. But she was, even then, able to learn in teams. She was persistent—dogged, perhaps. What might have been different for her had she had a more knowledgeable tutor in her writing conferences, or if she had had a reading journal in those early days of school? What does it take to provide teachers with classroom support for this kind of work? How much lobbying or protesting?

There are other issues that overwhelm school and teachers. One of my students, Mr. Edwards, was a fierce-looking man. I cannot remember why exactly, but he reminded me somehow of Long John Silver. His teacher from the semester before had also reported finding him frightening on first meeting. Coming from the streets of New Orleans, Mr. Edwards spent the better part of two semesters writing his "Life Store," and I learned from what he wrote that he "were a man at nine years old" and that he had learned to live "one way or the other." He reported that he had committed his first violent crime when he was newly on his own; and by the age of 14 a crime of passion sent him to jail. He ends this part of his life story saying, "As far as I could remember I knew more bad things than good."

By the end of the semester, he wrote, "I think that I have a second chance in life, and maybe something to offer to society and give back." In an interview, I asked him why he thought he was open to learning now when he had not been in the past. His answer was revealing. All through the time he spent in the penitentiary, he said, he was often goaded into fighting. The trigger for him was when one of the men would call out "Hey dumbbell Cholly [Charlie]."

Over the years, again and again, he was provoked into fighting. Punishment, no matter how harsh, was not enough to stop him. Surprisingly, he returned to school, and as an adult he discovered that he was not dumb—had never been dumb—and that he could learn and did do "some creative things." His discovery—that the link between insult and violence could be broken since he now knew he was not stupid—apparently brought him to "change my way of living in me."

What Now Is

These intensely personal and microstructural cases have something to say to us about the macrostructural problem of school failure. In the first half of this decade, California's prison population numbers 168,000, and the United States Department of Education found 65 percent are described as "illiterate." The nongraduation rate of minority students is high, but just how high is difficult to estimate as school districts rarely publicize those numbers. The story of the "Texas Miracle" illustrates this reluctance. Observers concluded "near-miraculous" results from the statewide use of the Texas Assessment of Academic Skills (TAAS) that began in 1990–91. Texas schools documented a 50 percent reduction in dropouts and improved test scores. However, Walt Haney (2000), an authority on test analysis, raised questions about the reliability and validity of the test, and also pointed out various statistical manipulations that kept many low-scoring students out of the sample. In short, even with efforts by teachers to "teach to the test," the bright promise of the Texas Miracle was dimmed: By the mid-1990s, 30 percent of youngsters were not passing TAAS and were thus "failing 9th grade, and by the turn of the century 50 percent of minority students had dropped out before high school graduation (Haney, 2000).

By and large, we are describing those from minority backgrounds, those who bring with them little economic capital and little cultural capital that schools respect. These things "just don't happen" to most children of middle-class values and backing.

Here, testing, schooled literacy, and adult illiteracy meet; micro and macro become one. Were there space, the theoretical explanation for the current state of affairs in modern institutions is a fascinating and hair-raising history (see Jim Collins, 1988). Suffice it to say that the history of literacy is very often the history of the "haves"; the history of illiteracy and the tests that measure it are very often the history of "have-nots." Considerable effort has gone into maintaining this kind of separation.

We take regular standardized testing for granted now, as schools test students constantly. Of course the tests are standardized, designed to offer a level playing field to all. We seek to normalize school performance and tend to see those who fall below the standard as not normal. The pity is that minority youngsters have so little vocabulary, as the educator E. D. Hirsch

(2001) wrote in a recent AFL-CIO publication. Thus the myth of the "deprived," "deficient" child and family reappears in a thousand subtle versions, although we never actually hear the words "deprived" or "deficient."

Yet, if other facts are assembled, they tell a different story. In an unpublished manuscript passed around among graduate students in 1987, James Collins described one study that shows readability formulas (which determine the words used in school tests) are most often created by selecting words widely known by middle-class speakers. Yet the same study cited findings to show that African American and working-class youngsters recognize the meaning of 302 and 293 words (respectively) that are unfamiliar to mainstream youngsters and to those who design measures of reading complexity. These vocabulary items of course rarely appear on these tests.

It may seem quite "natural" that English words familiar in the homes of minority communities do not appear as vocabulary items in school assessments and that the words chosen are those familiar to mainstream youngsters. I've learned to be cautious of "natural" assumptions like that, however; they often are the blinders of ethnocentrism and institutionalized racism. How "natural" might that taken-for-granted cultural fact seem in a society that actively seeks a level playing field?

These students are not abnormal. They are not unlearned. They are unschooled. If vocabulary is the problem, the shame (it seems to me) is that most classrooms do not drench *all* youngsters in a rich broth of language—not anymore. In true Catch-22 fashion, there is no time for teaching a love of language, for youngsters must prepare for standardized reading, grammar, and math tests. Increasingly, schools and teachers are forced to teach to the test.

What May Be

That is what is. But it is not as things are supposed to be, or need to be. We may have standardized tests, but we will never have standardized students who bring standardized languages into the classroom. As teachers dream about what we envision, strength arrives during dark times through classroom research. Wearing a research hat, we can begin to document the actual and not norm-based contours of language use across groups in our classrooms. Many speakers, like those I know best, live their lives below the radar screens, and their strengths as opposed to their substandard performances are undocumented. It is by building on those strengths that we can begin to guide them into the necessary school literacies.

I believe we will see more and more variants of literacies in and out of schools. By our show of interest, America's diverse language styles and discourses will appear out of the many enclaves across the country, from the Appalachian hollers, as Katherine Sohn (2006) shows, to West Side downtowns. We can study what learners bring to class from their own stock of knowledge, and experiment with teaching techniques that encourage interplay between standard lists of vocabulary and local expressions as synonyms or antonyms.

In institutions now, there may be little we teachers can do about examinations and scripted readers and worksheets. I can fight for funds to provide aides in classrooms—across grades and within advanced as well as remedial courses. I can ask, again and again and at ever-higher levels of bureaucracy, for teacher research time and pay, for better technology that sends students out with cameras to do social research in local neighborhoods (as Hull & James, 2007, have done). I can seek outside funds to set up the programs that I think might meet the needs of students. I can work within the school reform movement: For example, some giant high schools have been divided into smaller clusters that might improve connections between teachers and learners.

In Retrospect: Yesterday and Tomorrow

All of these moves help teachers influence the environments where they teach. But classroom research can better chart and affirm the varieties of language our students bring, and then help them develop the academic literacies they will need to succeed. This volume has described the detective work that starts as an "I wonder . . ." and winds up weeks, months, or years later with "I understand. . . ."

To further this research process for others, I have prepared an appendix, the "Guide to Classroom Research for Teachers," which describes classroom research processes so that teachers will know what to expect and how to proceed. This should limit the anxiety teachers too often suffer as they formulate questions, reflect on them, and locate answers.

Guide to Classroom Research for Teachers

Contents

Introduction

Our hope to better understand our schools and classrooms rests on the shoulders of the teachers. University professors who separate their research from teaching have had their go at our problems; they have offered answers that teachers have not always been able to use. Those who struggle in classrooms on the front lines, from pre-K to college, need to do their own research—and for this they need the help this "Guide" provides.

While there are many teacher-research texts—I mention a few of the best later in this section—most of them are complicated and assume teachers have the time to devote to an in-depth study of how research is done. This "Guide" recognizes that teachers are doing research on top of their regular teaching assignments, that much of their work is done on their own time, and that they need an outline of how to conduct research so that they can move quickly into their own classroom study. The previous chapters in this book are designed to offer examples of how research unfolds. This "Guide" offers hints and advice for teachers taking on their own work.

TRUSTING THE RESEARCH PROCESS

By 1990, research methods were changing. Ethnography, observation, and Clifford Geertz's (1979) "deep description" had become part of the landscape, and bit by bit classroom research appeared on the horizon. In the earlier period of classroom inquiry, individual teachers had often published the results of their work in the classroom as models to give teacher-researchers a starting point for projects. But I soon needed more. I needed to know what took place as the research unfolded and how others managed to get through the uncertainties and come out on the other side saying something about their classroom that mattered. Further, I wanted descriptions of the search and the excitement of the chase after answers. In the end, the excitement of the search has been what has kept me going year after year, project by project, and I envision this book as a way to convey it to others.

I want this "Guide" to be reassuring: For however clumsily one begins, or how deeply mired in confusion a project becomes, the research process unfolds in its own way. So long as the teacher who studies her classrooms wrestles honestly and earnestly with the unknowns, she can trust the process.

This "Guide" is not a feel-good recipe for doing nothing. The research process (like the writing process) has its own recursive and reliable phases, and the movement from one to the next can be plotted by taking note of the touchstones that signal the end of one phase, say collecting data, and the movement toward the next phase, in this case analysis. One may go one step forward and two steps back—that is, from analyzing data to collecting more data—or even back to square one, refining the focus. Moreover, the whole may repeat several times as each draft strengthens the outlines of the research and emphasizes the findings.

How This Guide Is Organized

The first section of this "Guide" concentrates on "Getting Started." Like the stories of Rose and Mark in Chapters 1 and 2, it underscores the contradictions we observe that call us to attention. It also gives more time to the difficulty of capturing the back-of-the-mind, tip-of-the-tongue questions.

> *Warning Number One:* The point of a classroom project may take a while to make explicit, and so it is well to be tolerant of these fits and starts.

At some point, earlier rather than later, research proceeds to a *focus*, and the second section of this "Guide", "Finding a Focus," describes the movement along this trajectory, mirroring the search detailed in Chapters 3 and 4. From the would-be teacher-researcher's perspective, Kelly's story (Chapter 3) illustrates just how complex the task of finding a focus may be. I was near the point of giving up when my work with Anthony (Chapter 4) helped me find my focus. I was then able to narrow the global "school failure" topic I had started with to a specific question: How does talk between a teacher and a student influence student writing?

> *Warning Number Two:* The first focus you settle on will probably be too big and will require much refinement. Do not be surprised at this. Trust the process. An awareness of something's importance, even if it is not yet explicit, is the only voice a teacher-researcher can hear.

What follows in the third and fourth sections will be "Collecting Ar-tifacts" and "Analyzing Artifacts," the next leg of the journey. Once your focus can be expressed in a clear question—such as, "Does talk influence writing?"—it will be obvious what you need to do next. In my case, in order to find out the links between talk and writing, data collection had to include exchanges between student and teacher as well as student writing. Deciding what evidence is necessary may continue into the later stages of the study. Research is a process that is recursive, a spiral along which we can go either up or down, not a series of tollgates that always funnel us forward.

When we collect data, we make decisions about what will best reveal an answer and what kinds of writings, tape-recordings, or videotapes will work best. However, sometimes even before we have the perfect ques-tion we already have noticed our curiosity about why certain students are reading certain books in their spare time or why others are not. Like life, sometimes research just happens.

Analysis is the search for meaning, and it is the heart of any research project. Historically, research has been divided into two camps, the quali-tative or quantitative, the verbal and the numerical. In accord with the shift away from "killer dichotomies," however, a current trend is the com-bination of these two types of analyses, and Chapters 6 and 7 show the power of using both.

The final section of this "Guide", "Writing It Up," argues for the teach-er-researcher's commitment to the completion of a project once it is begun. Reporting on whatever work has been done allows the researcher to pull together what she knows, to come to know it better, and to be able to make this knowledge public.

The first two sections end with what I have called "Warm-Ups," exer-cises designed for teachers at work on their research. They intend to help teachers see the familiar as strange. Seeing with new eyes often jump-starts and revitalizes research projects.

I.

Getting Started

There are many ways to begin. For me, the research process usually begins with a student who catches my interest. Above all, this "Guide" encourages you to find your own points of departure. No matter the ages of those we study and no matter the subject matter, the problem, or the distinctive understanding we come to, research journeys pass the same touchstones: starting out, finding a focus, collecting and analyzing data, and, at last, writing it up.

Reflecting

Beginning in about 1990, classroom research began to be recognized and regional or statewide conferences were devoted to it. Members of teacher-research groups began digging a supply line from classroom practice to the university's study of ideas about language, learning, literacy, or technology, and from there back again to classrooms.

In a research-based classroom, teachers are no longer "just" teachers. They are also witnesses to what passes before them. While a "just-teacher" may become angry, defensive, or curious about a student, a teacher-researcher considers the issue being raised and seeks a thread into a heretofore unseen classroom conflict or spurt of growth. Those inevitable moments we teachers have may become the rich soil where grow the questions that animate both career and profession.

It does not matter, as I see it, *why* a teacher makes classroom inquiry a part of her professional trajectory. Some teacher-researchers care greatly about their questions and yet care little about moving their findings out beyond their classroom or their school. Others argue that to strengthen teachers as professionals and classroom research as a "movement," we must publish in journals, speak at conferences, and raise grant funds for projects. Rather than an either-or choice between "action research" and fostering knowledge creation, classroom inquiry invites teachers to undertake many kinds of study.

What we do need to do, I think, is not judge but listen to one another: the publish-focused teacher, the empowered teacher who is making positive changes in her school, and the researcher who seeks to work as a change-agent for social justice. We need to listen to everyone who is trying to figure out what has not yet been resolved. When I pause while I am working, I read and reread the two quotes on the sign posted above my desk: "The real voyage of discovery consists not in seeking new landscapes but in having new eyes" (Marcel Proust), and "To be a beginner, always a beginner . . . " (Maria Rainer Rilke's advice to a young poet). For me, these quotes embody what teacher researchers do.

RESEARCH AS READING

Given that I have found a classroom moment that presents me with unknowns, I often turn to a library and find help from the reference librarian. For example, I recently noticed a 6th grader with a slight learning disability. Though he seemed to read well enough, he did not—could not, would not—write. I wondered about the source of the block: Was it physical, neurological, emotional, or cognitive? I recalled the titles of one or two works that concentrate on writers' blocks. Armed with this sort of hazy idea, I begin to track down who has had what to say about the subject.

Reading studies done by other classroom teachers can often cast light on our own worrisome questions. Manuals and handbooks written specifically for teachers studying their classrooms can help refine research processes. A recently published book by Elizabeth Chiseri-Strater and Bonnie Sunstein, *What Works: A Practical Guide for Teacher Research* (2006), gives suggestions for novice teacher-researchers. Equally helpful are *Teacher-Researchers at Work* (1999) by Marion MacLean and Marian Mohr, and (one of the classics in the field) *Teacher Research: From Promise to Power* (1990) by Leslie Patterson, John Stansell, and Sharon Lee.

Serving a similar purpose are those volumes and articles that offer descriptions of various research approaches: quantitative, historical, ethnographic, interpretive. In this volume's bibliography, Agar (1980), Rabinow and Sullivan (1979), Whiting and Whiting (1973), and Wolcott (1990) exemplify such useful documents. And when we ponder the articles in John Clifford and G. E. Marcus's *Writing Culture* (1986), we no longer assume that researchers are "invisible observers" but recognize ways their presences and interpretations affect the scenes they write about.

As teachers begin to wonder about the whys of what they see, the books and journals published in various research fields serve as another reading resource. The flow of information is vast—ranging from studies of culture to studies of the brain. In fact, as Steven Pinker (1997) argues, social sciences have begun to partner with the so-called "hard sciences," and research appears now by "sociobiologists" (pp. 44–45). Teacher-researchers will find in this vastness something that will support them and clarify what they do not understand.

The point is not that teacher-researchers read all this material before they begin. Instead, the classroom questions drive the engine while library materials merely deepen understandings of the issue.

RESEARCH AS OBSERVING

On the day a new semester starts, we are flooded with new information, material, artifacts, and data. In those first weeks, it is hard to separate out what is "ordinary" and what is "unusual." Once the semester is no longer new, we begin to see it all as comfortably predictable. This kind of predictability, however, runs counter to getting started on classroom research. So if we want to do classroom research, the *first step* is observing in a new way, observing as if we had never before considered which students come in late, who always sits in the very front row, and who never asks questions.

Typically, at the school day's end we pack for home the essays and the quizzes to be graded, the grade book, and the readings. We try to leave behind the contrasts and conflicts, the silent students as well as those who will not stop talking, the tensions between those who will not speak and those who mock others' lifestyles and language, and the students who suddenly understood what we have been teaching. We may not intend to, but those students come home with us. Perhaps while doing some household task, we mull over what blocks or speeds learning for some student and plan a lesson especially to draw him or her out or keep his or her attention. The next day, we watch that student and we may begin to see him or her in a new light.

Most teachers practice this kind of classroom research—reflecting on today's teaching, and considering ideas for tomorrow's teaching. However, since we often do not make any kind of record of it, we may not remember what we did for the next time, nor can we help a colleague who faces the same issue a year or a decade later. So the *second step* in getting started is to move from observing to recording. Write it down or lose it.

The *third step* in getting started is using schooltime differently. Teachers rarely leave school when students do. What if we took 15 minutes to makes notes about what happened today, about what matters personally and even passionately? That sort of reflecting may come in useful later.

A Teacher-Research Group

It may be more than worthwhile to set up a support group of teachers, no matter how few there are, who wish to do classroom research. In 1995 a Bay Area teacher-research group received funding to study what makes such a group successful. We learned that a cadre of teachers from a single school is the best model for a teacher-research group. Further, according to teachers' self-reports, a teacher-research group helps members to complete their classroom projects.

Another discovery the 1995 study made was that structured meetings led to shared contexts and greater involvement by the members; unstructured meetings had the opposite effect. Many routines are possible. The routine that we worked out in our "leaderless" group began with food and conversation, followed by a free-writing exercise in response to a provocative quotation or comment. Most of us read from our writing and we had a brief whole-group discussion. We then broke into groups of two or three for individual feedback on projects. The meeting ended after each group reported on the work they had done—a formal closure.

Getting Started Exercises

Warm-Up in Words

For starters, you are knocking at the door of your teaching. To see it as if from a stranger's perspective, seek always to look beyond the doorway into the heart of the place that keeps you alive and vital. Looking into that space, write, jot down thoughts on it, or discuss with a partner:

1. Your ideas today about classrooms, about research, and about classroom research
2. Your ideas today about the central influences you perceive on the students you see daily
3. Your ideas today about any unspoken tensions in your current classrooms (student-to-student, family-to-student, student-to-neighborhood, teacher-to-student)
4. Your ideas today about challenges and rewards you foresee as the result of adopting a classroom research project

Warm-Up in Images

Use newsprint to draw a familiar teaching space. Put in all the detail you can on this map: who sits where; the position of the desks; the coatroom, closet, or other areas of the room.

1. Based on this drawing, notice where you have left blanks. Perhaps you know a student's face but cannot remember a name.
2. Title the sketch.
3. Note one or more specific incidents that happened in one or more of the areas in this space. You need not write it in detail but your notations should identify why it was memorable.
4. Make an interpretation of the title and the space you have created as if you were again outside the teacher's door. Does the title reveal something about that space? Are there personal recollections—"Students X, Y, and Z's favorite reading spot"—or hints at the classroom's life? A sketch of five rows of desks labeled "My Classroom" tells little about what is going on in that space.

Warm-Up: Before and After

1. Draw the clock on the wall, with its hands marking the classroom hour you either dread most or look forward to the most. Again place the relevant furniture and learners around this clock. Put yourself in the picture. Where are you when it begins? What do you say?
2. What happens in that activity?
3. How does the room look after this activity? What are the students like at its conclusion? Where do the teacher and aides stand?
4. If you have learned anything new about what goes on beyond that door, write about one set of before and after snapshots. Seek to discover what exactly makes you so satisfied (or dissatisfied) with this time.

Warm-Up: Select a Spot

For as many days as possible, while your students are working independently or with partners or in groups, take out your pad of newsprint, announce to students that you will be doing your own work, and station yourself in one of the key positions in your room. Take 5 minutes—the whole 5 minutes—to examine the room from this vantage point. Notice:

1. One or two students at work and give all your attention for the full 5 minutes to them. You could also concentrate on the artifacts and activities in the room with which one or more students seem either engrossed or bored.
2. Characterize any members of the class as "types" you recognize: daydreamer, joker, quiet one, restless one, star. You may do it without names, using their place in class (left window, second seat, and so on). Observe one or more of these students over a week to check your first impressions. Has your mind changed about any of them? What triggered that reaction?

The Teacher's Record Book

For any of the sketches that seem to show you your classroom in a new way, record what you have witnessed. Some people are fond of using a designated journal or notebook. Others use any scrap of paper and then put it in a box or drawer where it can be retrieved. While you may not have a lot of time, make notes about what engaged your attention and what made you wonder.

To make your record useful as a research tool, put times and dates on everything you write. You may need this information later.

II.

Finding a Focus

The research process may begin for me with a person, but unless it moves quickly into why a certain student catches my interest, I will have nothing to say. It needs to shift quickly. And that shift from a subject or topic to something about the topic is the shift toward a focus.

An opportunity for a classroom research project is like a trailhead where dozens of possible directions call out. At the end of the broad trailhead path, narrower paths lead in different directions. The direction chosen will almost always illuminate some larger issues about which the teacher feels some passion. As a rule, moments in the daily round of teaching—moments when things do not go along as they should or when they go much better than we ever dreamed possible—make us aware of these bigger issues.

A sudden spark in which the whole class suddenly grasps a concept is only the tip of any particular unknown; what happened that ignited that class? What does it mean that one student never turns in written work without small drawings in the margin—are these drawings somehow part of his learning, or is he just playing around? What does it say to us about the way visual and verbal interact with each other?

To get on with a research project, limit the task; it is the only way to make it fun instead of onerous. If the topic seems overwhelming, it probably will be. If the multiple questions do not coalesce, pick one and drop whatever is not directly related. Your issue may be large, but ideally, the question should be narrow enough to finish in 6 months or a year. If it also opens the way into further research studies, that is all to the good. Do not wait for the Platonic ideal. Making a start is the bottom line.

Some questions contain warning signs that a topic will become too broad. Make the general wording concrete: replace "students" with a particular set of students (i.e., students in my precollegiate English class), a specific type of student (i.e., students who are repeating this course), or a certain number of students (i.e., four). Seek active verbs. "Will four students repeating precollegiate English improve their essays when they post them on a class website?" Further refinements or definitions, such as how to measure "improvement," can follow.

USING READING TO FIND A FOCUS

Just as the first section, "Getting Started," recommended reading what other researchers have written, so too your focus may become clearer by reading what other teachers have written. Consider the following two studies from the Bay Area Writing Project's first site-based teacher-research group: "An Activist Narrative: One Approach to Teaching Toni Morrison's *The Bluest Eye*" by E. Cole (2001–2002) and "Metacognitive Reading Strategies" by E. Filloy (2001–2002). Both of these studies appear in C. Tateishi's book *Bay Area Writing Project Teacher Research Program: Working Papers of Teacher Researchers (2001–2002)*.

The teacher-researchers in both of these studies remind us that it may take at least two tries to make the research topic small enough to handle in a busy year. Elena Cole, from Las Positas College in Livermore, California, studied her approach to teaching Toni Morrison's novel *The Bluest Eye*. Although other teachers tried to discourage her from teaching that novel, she had long believed that it could help students to "enter the text in ways they might not otherwise and emerge changed." Cole describes her attempts to study whether or not change occurred among her readers. The study she first undertook she dubbed a "failure," as she had been too quick to "do research," and in a rather heavy-handed way had set up pre- and postresponse measures that almost told students what to say and how to respond. The next semester, she "said less and listened more." Her crafting of an approach by which she now introduces the novel to the class seems to me a model of curriculum design.

Emily Filloy from the same teacher-research cadre examined the use of metacognitive strategies taught in reading class. Her focus, or question, was whether or not students used the strategies she emphasized in her class (e.g., asking themselves what they did or did not understand) in other classes. She found that 75 percent of the students reported using the strategies on their own in another class. The metacognitive strategies were transferring—at least in certain courses. Filloy also had several subquestions. She found, for example, that not all kinds of reading strategies were listed by students as useful. Some, such as the technique of predicting what would come next, were better understood than others, such as locating the cause of a comprehension problem and repairing it. She also notes that the survey she handed out to students mentioned that these strategies in reading were of little help in math, and suggested that math texts required further examination if metacognitive strategies were to be of aid to students in math classes.

Though some advise against it, I have found it useful to begin with a simple yes-no question such as "Do the metacognitive strategies we have practiced help students in other classes?" It offers a first peg to hang one's research hat on. Later on, subquestions can be further explored: "Which strategies do readers use most frequently? Which do they use less? What subjects lend themselves to these techniques? Which do not?" These questions could be extended: "Who uses these reading strategies most often? What do teachers in other classes explain about reading in their subject?" and so on.

The bibliography at the end of this book lists many resources that have shaped my thinking. My work might have looked entirely different had I not read "Toward a Social Cognitive Understanding of Problematic Writing" (1990), by Mike Rose and Glynda Hull, if Shirley Brice Heath had never spent 3 years doing ethnographic work in the Carolina Piedmont (see *Ways with Words* [1983]), and if John Gumperz had never examined interethnic miscommunication (see "Conversational Inference and Classroom Learning" [1981]).

A final set of resources that will be helpful to you in your research are those that describe the teacher's research processes, much as I am doing here but with varying terminologies and emphases. I have among my many papers an artifact called the "Research Log." Printed on a dot matrix printer, Marian Mohr (one of the first great leaders of classroom research) brought it to our teacher-research group in 1981. Mohr described the Research Log: "We begin the log at the first meeting of the group when we ask teachers to write what they notice in their classrooms that make them curious, something they would like to find out more about. As they write, they pinpoint the issues that have concerned them most." In the end, this log may be one of the best ways to follow one's own developing ideas. More recently, Mohr has published this information in *Teacher Researchers at Work* (MacLean & Mohr, 1999, pp. 12–19).

In almost every research group where teachers gather these days, there is discussion of protocols: protocols that help teachers begin Guided Reflections, Critical Incidents protocols, and so on. Much like the rubric a composition instructor passes out so that small writing groups work effectively, these materials eliminate the pointless chatter or the occasionally narcissistic "Oh yeah, now we've heard yours. What about mine?" They help, particularly when no one is especially practiced at eliciting clarifying questions and supporting comments. These materials originate, as I understand it, in a collaborative under the auspices of the Annenberg Institute's work for school change (see, for example the Web sites at www. lasw.org/protocols.html and www.annenberginstitute.org).

The Internet has many sites for teacher-researchers. For example, the website developed by Carnegie Teacher-Scholar programs illustrates in full detail the various ways individual teachers represent the work they and their student do. The sophistication of the technology all but seats us in the classrooms. These sites provide support for the solitary teacher-researcher.

ADVICE ON FOCUSING

Often, in order to find a focus, we must get under what we take for granted, beyond our knee-jerk response, "but of course test-scores tell us something." Any start is a good one; generating issues upon which teacher-researchers might focus can lead to endless lists. I find it much easier to begin not with a statement, such as "Skill-and-drill computer programs fail to improve student scores," but with a question: "Does a skill-and-drill computer program fail to improve student scores?" An even better question—for I do assume that skill-and-drill computer software will *not* be wildly successful—is: "What do skill-and-drill computer programs accomplish?" And here comes one of those caveats about the kind of question that decidedly will not do: Do not pursue a question with an answer you are already sure of, and that everyone else is sure of as well.

A second caveat is this: If a newly forming research group decides to set a single topic for everyone to concentrate on, that decision will work only through consensus—and such consensus must not achieved by ignoring a few murmurs of "Well, all right, if everyone else wants to." The group will suffer from a few members' lack of commitment, and that seething undercurrent will spread to general malaise, often recognizable by the fact that no one is doing any work in between group sessions. I have, in fact, seen research groups in which the facilitators become heavy-handed in steering group directions, and ultimately few or no projects at all are completed. With something as personal as one's own professional development, an assigned topic may not work. Some teachers are already on the trail of something they must follow to the end, and it may bear little resemblance to others' topics. In fact, some of the most informative groups I have been part of are those in which teachers from all grade levels are represented and a variety of topics pursued.

RUNNING WITH YOUR FOCUS

Once the point of the project is clear (and the teacher knows why it matters), the most enjoyable part of research (for me, at least) begins. Who will be involved in the study? When will it take place? How long will it last? All of these questions depend upon envisioning the procedures in a future moment of time. What will you do first, and second, and so on? All of this is part of developing a research design.

Given that the school year always goes faster than we expect, limit the task. How hard will it be to interview 25 students? Too hard; try two students and add more only if there is time. Examining test scores for, say, 30 students on three computer lessons is big but perhaps possible; *also* finding out how the 30 students felt about each of the three lessons through examining their journals and interviewing them is almost guaranteed to be such a daunting task that it cures the teacher of doing research forever thereafter. Again, limit the task. Remember, you can always divide a project in half and still have something worth reporting.

Teacher-researchers' classrooms are places where a million things that can be studied are identified and many possible reasons for each imagined. On the spur of the moment, a teacher may realize why a certain activity is not as effective as it can be, and within the space of a minute or two, she may make a tiny shift that improves engagement and learning. That kind of decision is, I believe, part of what the urban anthropologist Fred Erickson (1982) means when he speaks of the teacher as a "master of improvisation."

A teacher starts a teaching unit in motion, and after years of practice she knows by feel whether it is going well or badly. By listening, she adjusts the learning environment. That is what experts do, isn't it? Use personal know-how and intuition to ask the questions that matter and answer them before the learning ball drops.

For most of us, this expertise remains below the level of conscious awareness. It takes a while to make explicit to ourselves what we know. Once it is put into words, it can become public knowledge, available to all. Focusing a research question permits separating one thread from all the other questions and finding, eventually, how this strand connects to what will help in the classroom and what we want to know.

Finding a Focus Exercise

Warm-Up: Organizing Information

You may have notes that you've collected so far that, if organized, could reveal an emerging focus. To organize thinking to date, it helps to make use of a set of categories and to organize your observations within a system. Choose either of the following two systems, or create your own.

Classification Idea 1. One checklist I have used I adapted from the anthropologists Bea and John Whiting (1973). They offer the categories of *acts, persons, places,* and *"objects of group attention"* (p. 286). In applying these categories to classrooms, I see these examples:

Acts: Those things everyone in class undertakes such as homework (assigned by teacher, accomplished by students)

Persons: One or more persons involved (or not involved) in any activity

Places: One or more locales in which certain persons congregate or in which certain activities take place

Objects of group attention: Material objects such as an assigned text, a newsletter, notes taken in class (or even notes passed from student to student)

When I have sorted the observations into these piles, I notice that one or the other is full, another one has only one or two examples. The Whitings (1973) point out that by selecting one set of behaviors as a central focus of observation, it is possible to count how many times such and such an activity happens, or how often a student is left out of a small group, or what online sites students use for research tasks, and thus know the kinds of evidence that underlies one of the generalizations you hope to make in the study.

Classification Idea 2. A second organization system is suggested by Chiseri-Strater and Sunstein (2006) in their guide to teacher research. They recommend making four columns, labeling them *teaching practices, student learning or outcomes, school policies or politics,* and *curriculum* (p. 25). Find the central point among your musings and questions and place each under the appropriate heading. Which column has the preponderance of notes? Are there many "miscellaneous" notes? If so, do you need another category? Jot down any reflections suggested by your manipulation of observations.

At the earliest stage, classroom research projects are pilot studies— "first tries"—and will be guided primarily by a question and marked by tentativeness, not-knowing, and wondering. As you consider the advantages and disadvantages of various data, you are beginning to develop a research design. Keep it small and keep it simple. You will revisit what you want to know, what you need in order to know it, and what statement you want to make when you are finished with the study. Eventually, of course, a question ("Does student–teacher talk influence student essays?") evolves into a statement, or hypothesis ("Student–teacher talk influences student essay scores.") Chapters 4, 6, and 7 in this volume show that research questions, in all their complexity, develop along their own timelines.

If you can't learn everything you want to know about certain issues or questions in the next few months, what might help illuminate at least one part of it? A focus on just one part of an issue or problem lessens or prevents frustration. Most of us begin wanting to answer all the questions our subject suggests. We suffer from the (self-imposed) demand to set up research that will be "rigorous" and offer the "final answer." That may come in time, but for the moment, it is often a relief to concentrate on the collection of artifacts that intuitively seem interesting. Take time to reflect upon this data collection, upon what this student says about writing, or what those five journals reveal about a class field trip. When was the last time a teacher had a reason, an excuse, to do what she or he always wanted to do in the first place? That illusive question or focus often hides—in plain sight—among the artifacts that we just "happen" to save.

III.

Collecting Artifacts

*You learn something ("collect some data") then you try to make sense
out of it ("analysis") and see if the interpretation makes sense in light
of new experience ("collect more data") then you refine your interpretation ("more analysis") and so on. The process is dialectic, not linear.*
　　　　　　　　　　　　　　　　　—Michael Agar (1980, p. 9)

It is fortunate indeed when something in a classroom jumps out and demands to be studied. For most teachers, as soon as we wonder about how
students are relating to what we are teaching, we find ourselves hooked
on the search for new discoveries.

Gathering resources depends on what jumps out at you. One example
comes from a teacher-researcher who writes about her question:

> I was compelled to change the way I gave reading quizzes because
> of the poor grades on multiple-choice tests and the constant laments
> of one of the high-achieving students who says the tests "don't tell
> what she knows." I dropped the original quiz format and instead
> used an open-ended summary quiz, a test in which students could
> show more fully what they understand.

The data she collected included (1) the multiple-choice scores and
grades and (2) the new open-ended summary quiz scores and grades. An
unexpected observation was the students' engagement with each other as
they prepared for these quizzes. This classroom observation of collaboration between students led the teacher-researcher to a new focus. Her work
makes clear how classroom research spirals, how recursive this research-
ing process is, and how this year's questions ("What's the best way to
find out what my students know?") becomes next year's study. Questions
"jumped out" at this teacher, and she then used primary sources and the
observations she could collect and interpret in her search for answers.

But once artifact collection is under way, it can be very useful to
locate and at least skim through selected secondary sources that are relevant to your question and can further your thinking. A relevant list

of books and articles may shed light on your observations and other artifacts. It should grow as your thinking and your collecting of primary sources evolve.

The bibliography list will be especially valuable if you annotate each item; that is, write a short blurb about each resource on your list to remind you what the article is about and why you selected it. You can save the title and publishing facts in a file you keep handy on your desktop. Or you can start saving hard copies of these secondary sources in letter-size mailing envelopes. Label each ("writing conference studies," "case study research," "revision," and so on). I have often cut articles out of my professional journals or made copies of important chapters from books so that when I need to reread the article or double-check the accuracy of quotations I have the resource close at hand. Of course, saving electronic versions of texts in folders on your computer is the easiest way to keep them at hand.

OBSERVATIONS BY EYE AND EAR

Unless you are doing a bibliographic essay for later reference, the teacher's own experience—through observing, talking, reading student work, or otherwise gathering from the students who share the year with you—is the meat of a teacher's data collection.

Wherever teachers look there is something worth examining. The following list provides starting points but is not exhaustive. Observations work best if they are situated in actual classroom time. Reflections may yield more thoughtful notes after class time, but if you do not want them to become vague, take a few minutes to start the reflective write-up as closely as possible to the observations you are recording—and by all means date (month, day, and year) the documents.

Notice that these kinds of notes are not possible for the instructor in the moment of teaching. If you need an observer for something you are trying, ask another teacher to come in and record what she sees. (For suggestions, see the warm-up exercises in "Getting Started," which emphasize these kinds of note taking.)

Nothing can replace the teacher's own vision of her class, however, and a videotape unit is a wonderful way to get a view of your classroom while you are teaching. A student in class can operate the equipment with minimal training, and one or two well-chosen incidents will generate a huge amount of data. On the down side, this kind of observation gathering can leave you with nothing—minutes of capturing student heads with a muffled audio track. However, once you decide on what exactly you wish to collect, videotaping may be the best way to capture both what you see and what you hear: verbal and nonverbal interaction.

Whether you use pen and paper, a digital recorder, or videotapes, observations can be directed toward a single person on successive days, toward several people on successive days, or toward the whole group once or on successive days. By this point, the focus governs the gathering of artifacts.

When you are talking with (or interviewing) a student, it is possible to write what students say while simultaneously preparing to ask the next question, tweaking it if necessary. When you have a choice, use a tape recorder. It captures more information, records subtle nuances in the student's voice, and frees the interviewer to observe the student closely.

Stop. After you finish such a meeting, take 15 minutes to write in your reflective journal about what this interview taught you—and perhaps where your research has been and where you think it is going. Set this journal entry aside.

The Steps of Observation

The steps that follow are designed to bring your questions into focus. They assume you have at least an emerging area of interest that you can put into words. You need not know at the beginning what it is what you want to end up with, but it can serve to get you close (or closer) to that goal, to refine what you have.

Step 1: In your reflective journal or on sheets from a newsprint pad, write your current focusing question. If your focus is presently written as a statement, turn the statement into a question.

Step 2: Reflect on the question you have stated. In a journal entry or in a conversation with someone you trust, write or talk about what the question you have formulated means to you. As currently stated, is it centered on the cognitive, affective, or learning processes of one or more students, or on the social classroom context? Will its answer satisfy your curiosity about an area of interest you have explored before or wanted to explore? At the end of this reflection, you may want to refocus or tighten the question.

Step 3: Consider the practical issues your question raises. Is it answerable? Suppose that you have 6 months. How much time can you devote to the study of the question? Are the resources at hand?

Step 4: Define vague, ambiguous, or jargon-laden words in your question. It may lack a verb (a topic—a noun, without an active verb—cannot be a question). It may use vague terms; remember, any evaluative word, like "good" or "lazy" or "skilled reader," must be defined. It may use jargon—"in-group" terms.

Step 5: Assuming that the research question is something you want to study, make a list of the kinds of data you will gather (or have already gathered). Use the sample list provided below as a guide. Be sure that you have at least two different kinds of evidence to support your working hypothesis and any subquestions. To do this, circle the artifacts you have to use; if you have located other data, add them to this basic list.

WITHIN-SCHOOL ARTIFACTS

Observations (suggested by warm-up exercises, above)
Teachers' reflections on observations
Students' reflections on their own observations or on teachers' observations
Standardized tests
In-class quizzes or reports
Homework
Tape-recordings of students engaged in various activities
Interviews between teacher and one student recorded and transcribed
Tape-recorded and transcribed discussions among a small group of students with a student leader
Videotaped records of classwork or of activity during a lunch break or a between-classes break
Questionnaires
Surveys
Official data: cumulative folders
Course grades

OUTSIDE-OF-CLASSROOM BEHAVIORS

Students' projects, such as studies of their neighborhoods
Interviews with students when older or younger than they are now
E-mail and letter writing with students in another school, another town, or another country
Interview with elders
Compiling an oral history class book
Web sites and other Internet projects where students publish writings and post significant photographs or drawings

IV.

Analyzing Artifacts

So far, this "Guide" has taken us from trying to find the trail, to locating and strengthening a focus, and then to gathering evidence to support, elaborate, or explain that focus. Once we have gathered the evidence, we turn to analysis in order to understand—that is, interpret—what the data show. It is not until we apply our mind to our observations that our data collection becomes more than a big pile of scratch paper.

THE MANY SHAPES OF INTERPRETATION

Scientists have sought for decades to unify all the sciences within a single research method. They have sought an objective way to locate the "capital T" truth behind everyday practices. By removing all the "vague" names of ordinary language, they argued, we could think logically and deductively about things in the world. They hoped to reduce research to quantifiable, clearly defined, and logical categories and then use "objective" means to interpret the findings they had already arrived at logically.

Reality is not that cooperative. That kind of scientific objectivity was especially difficult for researchers in the social sciences. In the late 1980s, approaches to data collection that had been simmering under the surface for many years at last emerged. No longer seeking the global, researchers in the social sciences paid attention to the local. This interpretive approach had as its aim "not to uncover universals or laws but rather to explicate context and world" (quoted in Rabinov & Sullivan, 1979, p. 13). This approach also suggested a particular way of working: with rich and detailed descriptions, following any one activity—be it the fashions of women, the practices of education for girls, or a Balinese cockfight—to its place in the culture as a whole. Rather than reasoning deductively, these researchers worked inductively, reasoning from the seen to the unseen. They sought interpretation that served to point "beyond itself to the fundamental problems—theoretical, practical, and aesthetic—of human existence" (Rabinow & Sullivan, 1979, p. 18). Teacher-researchers appear on the scene at a particularly significant moment. We are no longer tied to either the first method (the quantitative) or the second (the qualitative).

Collecting and analyzing are not always separate, discrete activities. Sometimes they interweave. Something unexpected happens in your classroom—for example, a sudden rebellion, a class discussion that suddenly takes off and becomes a lively debate. What happened? What caused it? Whatever prompts an analysis, a four-step analytic process developed by David Tripp (1993; summarized by Hole & McEntee, 1999) becomes helpful. Step One, "What happened?" offers the teacher an opportunity to flesh out an event and describe the date, time, and other details. Step Two, "Why did it happen?" is the "beginning of reflection." Tripp recommends first examining the context for triggers that might be responsible for a particular event. We may discover that one event stands for a whole class of events, and those events may be characteristic of that school or that teacher. Although most reflection stops once it sees "the why of it, reflective practitioners need to look more deeply," to push the questioning a step further.

Step Three then asks teachers to stay with the seemingly insignificant event and consider "What might it mean?" Schools are busy places, and teachers' decisions are made in a split second. Why, then, do we make the choices that we do? We could have done something differently, but we did not. Why not? Talking or writing with that question before us points out teachers' responsibility. We need to be aware of more than what we will do Monday. In 1938 John Dewey wrote "the business of an educator is to see in what direction an experience is heading" (quoted in Hole & McEntee, 1999, p. 35). If the first three steps seem abstract, Step Four returns us to the everyday: "What are the implications for my practice?" Simon Hole and Grace McEntee say that deep reflection is "an entry into rethinking and changing practice" (Hole & McEntee, 1999, p. 36).

Hole and McEntee (1999) illustrate the analytic process by taking us through a "Critical Incident Protocol," an activity in which several teachers examine one teacher's classroom event. This example focuses on Simon and his experience with "the Geese and the Blinds" (pp. 35–36). In the first step of the protocol, our task is to record observations without judgment:

1. *What happened?* A teacher's note describes an incident in which "a student sees Canadian geese on the school lawn. Hopping from his seat, he calls out as he heads to the window for a better view. Within moments, six students cluster around the window. . . . When none of the students respond [to the teacher's call for attention], I walk to the window and lower the blinds."

In the second step, reflection begins as the teacher seeks explanations for what happened. A single event can be seen as part of a category of events:

2. *Why did it happen?* The teacher writes, "It's not hard to imagine why the students reacted to the geese. . . . Explaining my

reaction is more difficult. I knew [as I lowered the blinds that I missed] taking advantage of a learning opportunity. So why? . . . Two things stand out concerning that morning. First, the schedule. . . . Second, this is the most challenging class I've had in 22 years of teaching. I had trouble controlling the class, so I closed the blinds."

A reflective practitioner considers more deeply, however:

3. *What might it mean?* The teacher goes on to say, "Like a football quarterback, I often make bad decisions because of pressure. . . . Being a teacher means learning to live within that pressure, learning from the decisions I make, and learning to make better decisions."

A reflection like this could open into many directions regarding control, power, and authority in the classroom. But what is critical from this experience, Hole and McEntee state, is the action-oriented move into the final phase of guided reflection:

4. *What are the implications for my practice?* The teacher considers the source of his pressure, the administrative messages he has received that "I need to pay more attention to 'covering' the curriculum." But, he decides, "What is causing the lowering of the blinds stems from my not trusting enough in the process. Controlling the class in a fairly traditional sense isn't going to work in the long run. Establishing a process that allows the class to control itself will help keep the blinds up."

This analysis of a single event shows how the process of reflection begins. An extended research project might collect multiple observations of classroom control issues; seek experimental and theoretical insights into ways of understanding production learning behaviors; interview students, teachers, or administrators about this issue; and perhaps experiment with strategies designed to influence behavior.

There are two final reminders. First, do not forget that for an important project it is critical to set up a small "pilot" study. Write a set of interview questions, or a survey or questionnaire, and try these out with two or three students before you are ready to use them. You may want to try them with instructors as well. See what feedback they offer. Second, remember that the research process is recursive. We can revisit the project plan and timeline even at the eleventh hour and shift focus, or we can cut the job in half. The best cure for a bad case of being overwhelmed is to reduce the pile of data, even if it means putting on hold much rich information. By a strict limitation of focus, we often say more about less.

V.

Writing It Up

Few tasks are as hard, or as satisfying, as taking time to sit with your snapshots of students, your notes, your transcriptions, and your hunches. There was a time when I would have assumed that a final report would be a written manuscript. But today there are many more options: the conference talk (which needs references but no formal report); the digital story in which your documents are entered into a website and readers can walk through your ideas by various paths; and the face-to-face exchange, or sharing the story of your teaching in your faculty lunchroom or at a professional development gathering. Whatever form you choose, make a commitment to making your private reflections public knowledge. Unless research goes out into the world, others cannot build on it, or rebuild that part you did not get quite right. And no one ever gets everything 100 percent correct.

WRITING ADVICE: EASY TO GIVE, HARD TO FOLLOW

There is much to learn about writing up research. Wendy Bishop (1999) explains, in 250 pages, about "writing it down, writing it up, and reading it"—the "it" of course referring to research. Various manuals give detailed descriptions of how to write professional papers—whether for academic purposes (a thesis or dissertation) or for publication. Harry Wolcott (1990) offers an example of this kind of support. The advice I offer in the list that follows, however, is minimalist. It consists of what I gleaned from efforts at writing up my classroom studies, and what I wish I'd known before writing, rather than after. Wolcott's (1990) suggestions are even stronger (pp. 25–36).

1. Begin writing at the same time you start your project. Keep a well-packed research journal, and date everything you record. The more detailed your journal, the less you have to try to dredge up from memory when you reach the end. Believe me, in three months, without a date you will have no idea when such and so happened.

2. *Keep an annotated bibliography from the very beginning.* Include only the references you actually had in your hand. The forms for bibliography can be found in handbooks by the Modern Language Association (MLA), American Psychological Association (APA), or the *Chicago Manual of Style.*

If you are doing a presentation rather than a paper, you may want to identify other scholars in the field with whom you agree. For this purpose, it is courteous to prepare and hand out to your audience a bibliography of the three or four articles you found most helpful.

3. *Keep a record of what you hand out in class, when, and to whom.* Who had this activity yesterday and who will have that one tomorrow? All of these details will disappear into your catchall memory, and you will never be able to retrieve them later exactly as they are at the moment of occurrence.

4. *File your stacks of papers (i.e., data) for easy retrieval.* Everyone creates order in a different way, but, if at all possible, begin filing your data after the first interview you complete, or the first set of scores or papers. If you have not yet done so, create a special file for your teaching logs or research journals and try reading them from the earliest to the latest entries or vice versa. Do any changes over time become clear?

5. *Make sure you have written permissions from those who provide you with data.* If students are under the age of 18, the permission slips must be signed by parents.

6. *Take time to reflect.* With your research question and your data and research logs fresh in mind, let your reflections become a focused free writing. That piece of writing will hold many of your key ideas—in fact, probably all of them. The data, then, bring to life the point your reflection considers.

Now may be the time to compose a first draft. If your focused free writing did not provide shape, begin with your research question, then follow your notes. Remember that for every idea you need at least one example. Try to put as much in the first go-round as you can. It can always be cut. If you still cannot get going, start writing about the moment you now see as marking the beginning of your study.

As you are deciding how much to include and what to leave out, make sure that whatever point you are making about your classroom is seen from at least two perspectives. In Maybell's story in Chapter 8, a teacher's

log, interviews, and student writing all point toward the once-silent Maybell coming into her own voice. Using more than one data source in this
way is called *triangulation*: verifying what is seen from one angle by making the same point with different kinds of data. This strategy gives your
ideas as many legs to stand on as possible.

REPORT FORMATS

But how do I get started? Stripped to their bones, I have read (and written)
two main kinds of reports: the problem paper and the case study. They
both fit within the anecdotal or description/narration form or genre. They
both tell a story. After deciding how (or if) you can make the story of your
research, consider the two following ideas:

Problem Paper

What I am calling the problem paper usually begins with the first
strong impression you had, the impression that led you to write about a
particular topic in the first place. Practicing writing such "leads" (for that
is what they are—a way of capturing your readers' interest and empathy)
is a good idea, especially when you have one or two readers who can help
you tease out the meanings.

Teacher-researchers often start with something that is going a little
wrong—or a little right—in their classrooms. With the teacher's increased
awareness, there may be a gradual shift, ultimately, we hope, toward ongoing change and growth.

At other times, teacher research uncovers some institutional wrong
which cannot be overcome. The lead may simply describe the genesis of
one's awareness of an issue: "One day, I was going along business as usual
when I opened the classroom door to find . . ." Kathryn Herr (1999), a
teacher-researcher in a small private school, reports on a year-long study
that came up with some very hard facts about institutional racism, facts
no one wanted to see. We share her struggle with the problem, the hidden
racisms of institutions (a familiar refrain), and at the same time she opens
the question as to whether or not classroom research can have results, can
be turned to fit the activist's hand.

On this political issue, Vincent Crapanzano (1986) offers important reminders: Writings by ethnographers (including teacher-researchers) have
the power to speak to your reader(s) and, in a sense, speak in the place of
those described. In writing about classroom experiences, watch that you
do not cast yourself in the starring role and present students as generic

stereotypes. Also, do not take away the students' own voices. There are two litmus tests for this ethical issue. One is asking yourself if you are comfortable showing your writing to your students (Crapanzano, 1986, p. 70). If you might be embarrassed about a description or comment, think about recasting that sentence. The other is to look to your pronouns. If you use pronouns of "they" and "them" to refer to students, check to make sure you have not placed your students in passive, "underling" postures, as if you are speaking over their heads to another, more sophisticated, listener (pp. 68–76). Would the passage sound more inclusive if you spoke of "our classroom" when possible?

Case Study

We know Jean Piaget's theory of cognitive development came about in large part through the observation of one or two children, his own. It is not the amount of data you use that matters, but the ideas that hold it together. Great work can originate from a very small sample indeed.

Case study research means following the behavior(s) of one or two people with a magnifying glass held steady. As Glenda Bissex defines this form of teacher research, case studies are the "observation of individuals in their normal environment" (Bissex & Bullock, 1987, p. 8). She points out a particular strength of case studies—that they encourage us to look for what is unique and to understand the individual in the context that plays a critical role in shaping his or her behavior. Further, although quantitative research has held pride of place for a long time, the multiple factors that affect outcomes have led teacher-researchers to ask, "What is the good of counting test scores if we are not sure we have counted critical influences that matter?"

Glenda Bissex (in Bissex & Bullock, 1987) reminds us also—and it has certainly been borne out in several of the studies reported here—that if the teacher's self-reflections are a part of the study, it is difficult to disguise both bad practice and bias. In fact, as she says, one of the best sources of professional development is listening to a tape-recording in which the teacher hears herself interrupting and silencing students again and again. That behavior, she points out, will change by the time that teacher has transcribed even part of that taped conversation.

A well-planned case study may rely on observations and be fleshed out by reflections about them. I underscore, for myself, that word *reflection*. Unless I note the impact of a particular event almost as soon as it happens, I will be unable to re-create later the meaning of that particular glimpse into student behavior or event. And woe to the classroom researcher who never links what is seen with what it means!

Finding Our Form

When teachers gather, they tell stories about classroom life many nonteachers do not understand. These anecdotes are filled with meaning that others may not hear. What about Rose? What about all the other students whose tales we know best? How can their learning be shared with others?

When we are ready to write what we know, how can we convey to others the personal and professional meanings we make? What rhetorical form can we use? Narratives do not have a good reputation in academia. Joy Ritchie and David Wilson (2000), recognizing that "telling stories" has been regarded as inferior to analytic, "objective," and scientific journal articles, argue instead that narrative can invite and allow teachers to "resist and revise those scripts" of gender, class, and sexuality that we neither made nor chose and which lock us into our personal and professional identities (pp. 1–2).

Narrative may be a fine vehicle for reflection. In considering the theory of genre, the genre of story may be, as Patricia Stock (2001) calls it, "our form." It is a discourse form that frequently serves teachers well. In story, we can embed all that we know and care about. For a first draft, a teacher-researcher could do worse than string together a few important anecdotes that relate what happened over time, or those that show what becomes increasingly important. You can state the problem from a more or less objective view, as news reporters do. Report on what other researchers or reporters mention in their articles, relate how you went about your research, list your findings, and then discuss their importance. You can describe a single student in a case study, contrast two students (as I do in Chapters 6 and 8), or select a sample of students from the full class. You can even plan a study with the whole class. In short, there are as many ways to write up your findings as there are findings to be found. And it is only through such write-ups that classroom teachers can build a proper supply line, one that flows not only from the university and into the classroom, but also from the classroom and back to the university.

References

Abrahams, R., & Gay, G. (1972). Talking Black in the classroom. In R. Abrahams & R. Troike (Eds.), *Language and cultural diversity in American education* (pp. 200-208). Englewood Cliffs, NJ: Prentice-Hall.

Abrahams, R., & Troike, R. (Eds.). (1972). *Language and cultural diversity in American education*. Englewood Cliffs, NJ: Prentice-Hall.

Agar, M. (1980). *The professional stranger: An informal guide to ethnography.* New York: Academic Press.

Allen, R. I. (1966). Writing is a "second language." *English Journal, 55,* 739-746.

Atwell, N. (1987). Everyone sits at a big desk: Discovering topics for writing. In D. Goswami & P. Stillman (Eds.), *Reclaiming the classroom: Teacher research as an agency for change* (pp. 178–187). Upper Montclair, NJ: Boynton/Cook.

Austin, J. L. (1962). *How to do things with words.* Oxford: Clarendon Press.

Ausubel, D. (1964). How reversible are the cognitive and motivation effects of cultural deprivation? *Urban Education, 1,* 16-38.

Ball, A. F. (2000). Teachers' developing philosophies on literacy and their use in urban schools: A Vygotskian perspective on internal activity and teacher change. In C. D. Lee & P. Smagorinsky (Eds.), *Vygotskian perspectives on literacy research: Constructing meaning through collaborative inquiry* (pp. 226–255). Cambridge: Cambridge University Press.

Baratz, J., & Baratz, S. (1972). Black culture on Black terms: Rejection of the social pathology model. In T. Kochman (Ed.), *Rappin' and stylin' out: Communication in urban Black America* (pp. 3-18). Urbana: University of Illinois Press.

Barth, F. (Ed.). (1998). *Ethnic groups and boundaries: The social organization of culture difference.* Long Grove, IL: Waveland Press. (Original work published in 1969)

Bartholomae, D. (1983). Writing assignments: Where writing begins. In P. Stock (Ed.), *Fforum* (pp. 300–312). Upper Montclair, NJ: Boynton/Cook.

Bartholomae, D. (1986). Words from afar. In A. Petrosky & D. Bartholomae (Eds.), *The teaching of writing* (pp. 1-7). Eighty-fifth yearbook of National Society for the Study of Education. Chicago, IL: National Society for the Study of Education.

Bateson, G. (2000). *Steps to an ecology of mind.* Chicago: University of Chicago Press. (Original work published 1972).

Bereiter, C., & Engelmann, S. (1966). *Teaching disadvantaged children in the preschool.* Englewood Cliffs, NJ: Prentice Hall.

Berthoff, A. (1981). *The making of meaning: Metaphors, models, and maxims for writing teachers.* Portsmouth, NH: Boynton/Cook.

Bishop, W. (1999). *Ethnographic writing research: Writing it down, writing it up, and reading it.* Portsmouth, NH: Boynton/Cook.

Bissex, G., & Bullock, R. (Eds.). (1987). *Seeing for ourselves: Case-study research by teachers of writing.* Portsmouth, NH: Heinemann.

Bizzell, P. (1986). Composing processes: An overview. In A. Petrosky & D. Bartholomae (Eds.), *The teaching of writing* (pp. 49–70). Eighty-fifth yearbook of the National Society for the Study of Education. Chicago: National Society for the Study of Education.

Bleich, D. (1989). Reconceiving literacy: Language use and social relations. In C. Anson (Ed.), *Writing and response: Theory, practice, and research* (pp. 15–36). Urbana, IL: National Council of Teachers of English.

Bogdan, D., & Straw, S. B. (Eds.). (1990). *Beyond communication: Reading comprehension and criticism.* Portsmouth, NH: Boynton/Cook.

Bowles, S., & Gintis, H. (1976). *Schooling in capitalist America: Educational reform and the contradictions of economic life.* New York: Basic Books.

Brooke, R. (1991). *Writing and sense of self: Identity negotiation in writing workshops.* Urbana, IL: National Council of Teachers of English.

Brown, P., & Levinson, S. (1987). *Politeness: Some universals in language usage.* Cambridge: Cambridge University Press. (Original work published 1978)

Bruffee, K. A. (1986). Social construction, language, and authority of knowledge: A bibliographical essay. *College English, 48*(8), 773–789.

Cayer, R. L., & Sacks, R. K. (1979). Oral and written discourse of basic writers: Similarities and differences. *Research in the Teaching of English, 13*(2), 121–128.

Cazden, C. (1972). *Child language and education.* New York: Holt, Rinehart, & Winston.

Chall, J. (1967). *Learning to read: The great debate.* Fort Worth, TX: Harcourt-Brace.

Chall, J. (1996). American reading achievement: Should we worry? *Research in the Teaching of English, 30*(3), 303–310.

Chiseri-Strater, E., & Sunstein, B. (2006). *What works: A practical guide for teacher research.* Portsmouth, NH: Heinemann.

Chomsky, N. (1965). *Aspects of the theory of syntax.* Cambridge, MA: MIT Press.

Chomsky, N. (1967). A review of B. F. Skinner's verbal behavior. In L. Jakobovits & M. Miron (Eds.), *Readings in the psychology of language* (pp. 142–179). Englewood Cliffs, NJ: Prentice-Hall.

Cicourel, A. (1974). Introduction. In A. Cicourel, K. Jennings, S. Jennings, K. Leiter, R. MacKay, H. Mehan, & D. Roth (Eds.), *Language use and school performance* (pp. 2–16). New York: Academic Press.

Clifford, J., & Marcus, G. E. (Eds.). (1986). *Writing culture: The poetics and politics of ethnography: A school of American research advanced seminar.* Berkeley: University of California Press.

Cole, E. (2000–2001). An activist narrative: One approach to teaching Toni Morrison's *The bluest eye.* In C. Tateishi (Ed.), *Bay Area Writing Project teacher research program: Working papers of teacher researchers* (pp. 54–59). Berkeley: University of California.

Cole, M., & Bruner, J. (1971). Cultural differences and inferences about psychological processes. *American Psychologist, 26*(10), 867–876.

Collins, J. (1986). Differential instruction in reading groups. In J. Cook-Gumperz (Ed.), *The social construction of literacy* (pp. 117–137). New York: Cambridge University Press.

Collins, J. (1988). *Hegemonic practice: Literacy and standard language in public education.* Berkeley: University of California.

Collins, J., & Michaels, S. (1986). Speaking and writing: Discourse strategies and the acquisition of literacy. In J. Cook-Gumperz (Ed.), *The social construction of literacy* (pp. 207–223). New York: Cambridge University Press.

Cook-Gumperz, J. (1986). *The social construction of literacy.* New York: Cambridge University Press.

Cooke, B. (1972). Non-verbal communication among Afro-Americans. In T. Kochman (Ed.), *Rappin' and stylin' out: Communication in urban Black America* (pp. 32–64). Urbana: University of Illinois Press.

Crapanzano, V. (1986). Hermes' dilemma: The masking of subversion in ethnographic description. In J. Clifford & G. Marcus (Eds.), *Writing culture: The poetics and politics of ethnography* (pp. 51–76). Berkeley: University of California Press.

Crystal, D. (1976). *Prosodic systems and intonation in English.* Cambridge: University of Cambridge Press.

Davis, F. (1944). Fundamental factors of comprehension in reading. *Psychometrika, 9,* 185–197.

Delpit, L. (1986). Skills and other dilemmas of a progressive Black educator. *Harvard Education Review, 56*(4), 379–385.

Delpit, L. (1988). The silenced dialog: Power and pedagogy in educating other people's children. *Harvard Educational Review, 58*(3), 280–298.

Deutsch, M. (1967). The disadvantaged child and the learning process. In M. Deutsch (Ed.), *The disadvantaged child* (pp. 34–89). New York: Basic Books.

Dewey, J. (1938) *Experience and education.* New York: Macmillan.

Elbow, P. (1973). *Writing without teachers.* New York: Oxford University Press.

Erickson, F. (1976). Gate-keeping encounters: A social selection process. In P. Sanday (Ed.), *Anthropology and the public interest* (pp. 111–143). New York: Academic Press.

Erickson, F. (1982). Classroom discourse as improvisation: Relationships between academic task structure and social participation structure in lessons. In L. C. Wilkenson (Ed.), *Communicating in the classroom* (pp. 153–181). New York: Academic Press.

Erickson, F., & Schultz, J. (Eds.). (1982). *The counselor as gatekeeper: Social and cultural organization of communication in counseling interviews.* New York: Academic Press.

Fader, D. (1972). *The naked children.* New York: Bantam Books.

Filloy, E. (2001–2002). Metacognitive reading strategies: Where do they go after reading class? In C. Tateishi (Ed.), *Bay Area Writing Project teacher research program: Working papers of teacher researchers.* Berkeley: University of California.

Fish, S. (1980). *Is there a text in this class?* Cambridge, MA: Harvard University Press.

Flower, L. (1987). Thinking aloud while you write. In *The role of task representation in reading to write* (pp. 31–32). *Pittsburgh, PA:* Carnegie-Mellon Institute.

Flower, L., & Hayes, J. (1981). A cognitive process theory of writing. *College Composition and Communication, 32,* 365–387.

Frazier, A. (Ed.) (1964). A research proposal to develop the language skills of children with poor background. In *Improving English skills of culturally different youth in large cities.* Washington, DC: U.S. Office of Education.

Freedman, S. (1976). *The impromptu conference.* Paper presented at the annual meeting of the National Council of Teachers of English, Chicago, IL.

Freire, P. (2000). *Pedagogy of the oppressed.* (30th anniversary ed.; M. B. Ramos, Trans.). New York: Continuum. (Original work published 1970)

Furnivall, J. S. (1944). *Netherlands India: A study of plural economy.* Cambridge: Cambridge University Press.

Garrison, R. H. (1974, Spring). One-to-one: Tutorial instruction in freshman composition. *New Directions for Community Colleges, 5,* 55–84.

Gee, J. (1991). *Social linguistics and literacies: Ideology in discourses* (2nd ed). London: Falmer Press.

Geertz, C. (1979). Deep play: Notes on the Balinese cockfight. In P. Rabinow & W. Sullivan (Eds.), *Interpretive social science: A reader* (pp. 181–224). Berkeley: University of California Press.

Gere, A. R. (1986). Teaching writing: The major theories. In A. Petrosky & D. Bartholomae (Eds.), *The teaching of writing* (pp. 30–48). Eighty-fifth yearbook of the National Society for the Study of Education. Chicago: National Society for the Study of Education.

Goffman, E. (1963). *Behavior in public places: Notes on the social organization of gatherings.* New York: Free Press.

Goodman, K., & Goodman, Y. (1967). Reading: A psycholinguistic guessing game. *Journal of the Reading Specialist, 4,* 126–135.

Goody, J. (1977). Evolution and communication. In *The domestication of the savage mind* (pp. 1–18). Cambridge: Cambridge University Press.

Gottesman, I. (1968). Biogenetics of race and class. In M. Deutsch, I. Katz, & A. Jensen (Eds.), *Social class, race, and psychological development* (pp. 11–53). New York: Holt, Rinehart, and Winston.

Gough, P. B. (1976). One second of reading. In H. Singer & R. Ruddell (Eds.), *Theoretical models and processes of reading* (2nd ed.). Newark, DE: International Reading Association.

Grice, P. (1975). Logic and conversation. In P. Cole & J. Morgan (Eds.), *Syntax and semantics: Speech acts* (pp. 41–58). New York: Academic Press.

Gumperz, J. (1981). Conversational inference and classroom learning. In J. Green, & C. Wallat (Eds.), *Ethnography and language in educational settings* (pp. 161–209). Norwood, NJ: Ablex.

Gumperz, J. (Ed.). (1982a) *Discourse strategies.* Studies in Interactional Sociolinguistics. Cambridge: Cambridge University Press.

Gumperz, J. (Ed.). (1982b). *Language and social identity.* Studies in Interactional Sociolinguistics. Cambridge: Cambridge University Press.

Gumperz, J., & Herashimchuk, E. (1972). Conversational analysis of social meaning. In R. Shuy (Ed.), *Sociolinguistics: Current trends and prospects.* Georgetown University Round Table on Language and Linguistics. Washington, DC: Georgetown University Press.

Gumperz, J., Kaltman, H., & O'Connor, M. (1984). Cohesion in spoken and written discourse: Ethnic style and the transition to literacy. In D. Tannen (Ed.), *Coherence in spoken and written discourse* (pp. 3–20). Norwood, NJ: Ablex.

Halliday, M. A. K. (1985). *Spoken and written language.* Victoria, Australia: Deakin University Press.

Haney, W. (2000). The myth of the Texas miracle in education. *Education Policy Analysis Archives, 8*(41). Retrieved November 10, 2006, from: http://www.epaa.asu.edu/epaa/v8n41

Hannerz, U. (1969). *Soulside: Inquiries into ghetto culture and community.* New York: Columbia University Press.

Harris, J. (1991). After Dartmouth: Growth and conflict in English. *College English, 53*(6), 631–647.

Heath, S. B. (1983). *Ways with words: Language, life, and work in communities and classrooms.* Cambridge: Cambridge University Press.

Heath, S. B. (1989a). Oral and literate traditions among Black Americans living in poverty. *American Psychologist, 44*(2), 367–383.

Heath, S. B. (1989b). Talking the text in teaching composition. In S. de Castell, A. Luke, & C. Luke (Eds.), *Language, authority, and criticism: Readings on the school textbook* (pp. 109–122). London: Falmer Press.

Herr, K. (1999). Unearthing the unspeakable: When teacher research and political agendas collide. *Language Arts, 77*(1), 10–17.

Herrnstein, R., & Murray, C. (1994). *The bell curve: Intelligence and class structure in American life.* New York: Simon & Schuster.

Hill, C. (1977). A review of the language deficit position: Some sociolinguistic and psycholinguistic perspectives. *IRCD Bulletin, 12*(4), 1–13.

Hirsch, E. D. (1988). *Cultural literacy: What every American needs to know.* New York: Random House.

Hirsch, E. D. (2001). Overcoming the language gap: Make better use of literacy time block. *American Educator, 5*(2), 4, 6–7.

Hole, S., & McEntee, G. (1999). Reflection is at the heart of practice. *Educational Leadership, 56*(8), 34–37.

Holt, J. (1965). *How children fail.* New York: Dell.

Hull, G. (1986). Acts of wonderment: Fixing mistakes and correcting errors. In D. Bartholomae & A. Petrosky (Eds.), *Facts, artifacts, and counterfacts: Theory and method for a reading and writing course* (pp. 193–226). New York: Heinemann.

Hull, G., & James, M. A. (2007). Geographies of hope: A study of urban landscapes and a university-community collaborative. In P. O'Neill (Ed.), *Blurring boundaries: Developing writers, researchers, and teachers—A tribute to William L. Smith.* Cresskill, NJ: Hampton Press.

Jacobs, S., & Karlinger, A. (1977). Helping writers to think. *College Composition and Communication, 38*, 489–505.

Jensen, A. (1968). Social class and verbal learning. In M. Deutsch, I. Katz, & A. Jensen (Eds.), *Social class, race, and psychological development* (p. 115–174). New York: Holt, Rinehart, & Winston.

Jensen, A. (1969). How much can we boost IQ and scholastic achievement? *Harvard Educational Review, 39*, 1–123.

Jensen, A. (1973). The role of verbal mediation in mental development. In *Educational differences* (pp. 131–166). London: Methuen.

Johnson, K. (1972). The vocabulary of race. In T. Kochman (Ed.), *Rappin' and stylin' out: Communication in urban Black America* (pp. 140–151). Urbana: University of Illinois Press.

Jupp, T., Roberts, C., & Cook-Gumperz, J. (1978). Language and disadvantage: The hidden process. In J. Gumperz (Ed.), *Language and social identity* (pp. 232–257). Cambridge: Cambridge University Press.

Katz, I. (1967). Review of evidence relating to effects of desegregation on the intellectual performance of Negroes. In A. H. Passow (Ed.), *Education of the disadvantaged*. New York: Holt, Rinehart, & Winston.

Keiser, R. L. (1972). Roles and ideologies. In T. Kochman (Ed.), *Rappin' and stylin' out: Communication in urban Black America* (pp. 349–369). Urbana: University of Illinois Press.

Kochman, T. (1972). Toward an ethnography of Black American speech behavior. In *Rappin' and stylin' out: Communication in urban Black America* (pp. 241–264). Urbana: University of Illinois Press.

Kohl, H. (1967). *Thirty-six children*. New York: New American Press.

Labov, W. (1972a). The logic of non-standard English. In *Language in the inner city: Studies in the Black English vernacular* (pp. 201–240). Philadelphia: University of Pennsylvania. (Original work published in 1969)

Labov, W. (1972b). The transformation of experience in narrative syntax. In *Language in the inner city: Studies in the Black English vernacular* (pp. 354–396). Philadelphia: University of Pennsylvania Press. (Original work published in 1969)

Labov, W. (1972c). Some sources of reading problems for speakers of the Black English vernacular. In *Language in the inner city: Studies in the Black English vernacular* (pp. 3–35). Philadelphia: University of Pennsylvania Press. (Original work published in 1969)

Lakoff, R. (1979). *Expository writing and the oral dyad as points on a communicative continuum: Writing anxiety as the result of mistranslation.* Unpublished manuscript, University of California, Berkeley.

Lambert, W., Hodgson, G., Gardener, R., & Filenbaum, C. (1960). Evaluational reactions to spoken languages. *Journal of Abnormal and Social Psychology, 60,* 44–51.

LeClair, T. (1981, March). "The language must not sweat": A conversation with Toni Morrison. *The New Republic, 184,* 25–29.

Lee, C. (2000). Signifying in the zone of proximal development. In C. Lee & P. Smagorinsky (Eds.), *Vygotskian perspectives on literacy research* (pp. 191–225). Cambridge: Cambridge University Press.

Lee, C., & Smagorinsky, P. (Eds.). (2000). *Vygotskian perspectives on literacy research*. Cambridge: Cambridge University Press

Leiter, K. C. (1974). Ad hocing in the schools: A study of placement practices in the kindergartens of two schools. In A. Cicourel, S. H. M. Jennings, K. H. Leiter, K. C. W. MacKay, H. Mehan, & D. R. Roth (Eds.), *Language use and school performance* (pp. 17–73). New York: Academic Press.

Levy, G. (1970). *Ghetto school: Class warfare in an elementary school.* New York: Pegasus Books.

Lewis, L. (1970). Culture and social interaction in the classroom: An ethnographic report. *Working Paper of the Language-Behavior Research Laboratory, No. 38.* Berkeley: University of California.

Light, R. (1972). Language arts and minority group children. In R. Abrahams & R. Troike (Eds.), *Language and cultural diversity in American education* (pp. 9–15). Englewood Cliffs, NJ: Prentice-Hall.

Lord, A. B. (1960). The formula. In *The singer of tales* (pp. 30–67). Cambridge: Cambridge University Press.

Lunsford, A. (1991). The nature of composition studies. In E. Lindeman & G. Tate (Eds.), *An introduction to composition studies* (pp. 3–14). New York: Oxford University Press.

Luria, A. R. (1976). *Cognitive development: Its social and cultural foundations.* Cambridge, MA: Harvard University Press.

MacLean, M., & Mohr, M. (1999). *Teacher-researchers at work.* Berkeley, CA: National Writing Project.

McDavid, R. I., & McDavid, G. (1972). The relationship of the speech of American Negroes to the speech of Whites. In R. Abrahams & R. Troike (Eds.), *Language and cultural diversity in American education* (pp. 213–219). Englewood Cliffs, NJ: Prentice-Hall. (Original work published in 1951)

McDermott, R. (1976). The explanation of minority school failure, again. *Anthropology and Education Quarterly, 18,* 361–364.

Macrorie, K. (1970). *Telling writing* (2nd ed.). Rochelle Park, NY: Hayden Press.

Mehan, H. (1974). Accomplishing classroom lessons. In A. Cicourel, K. Jennings, S. Jennings, K. Leiter, R. MacKay, H. Mehan, & D. Roth (Eds.), *Language use and school performance* (pp. 76–143). New York: Academic Press.

Melmed, P. (1973). Black English phonology: The question of reading interference. In J. Laffey & R. Shuy (Eds.), *Language differences: Do they interfere?* (pp. 70–85). Newark, DE: International Reading Association.

Michaels, S. (1986). Narrative presentations: An oral preparation for literacy with first graders. In J. Cook-Gumperz (Ed.), *The social construction of literacy* (pp. 94–116). Cambridge: Cambridge University Press.

Mitchell-Kernan, C. (1974). *Language behavior in a Black urban community* (Rev. ed.). Monographs of the Language Behavior Research Laboratory, No. 2. Berkeley: University of California.

Moats, L. C. (2001). Overcoming the language gap: Invest generously in teacher professional development. *American Educator, 25*(2), 5, 8–9.

Moffett, J. (1968). *Teaching the universe of discourse.* Boston: Houghton-Mifflin.

Naremore, R. (1971). Teachers' judgments of children's speech: A factor analytic study of attitudes. *Speech Monographs, 38,* 17-27.

Naroll, R. (1964). On ethnic unit classification. *Current Anthropology, 5*(4), 283–291.

Newkirk, T. (1997) *The performance of self in student writing.* Portsmouth, NH: Boynton/Cook, Heinemann.

Ogbu, J. (1974). *The next generation: Ethnography of education in an urban neighborhood.* New York: Academic Press.

Ogbu, J. (1978). *Minority education and caste: The American system in cross-cultural perspective.* New York: Academic Press.

Ogbu, J. (n.d.) *The origins of human competence.* Unpublished manuscript, University of California, Berkeley.

Patterson, L., Stansell, J., & Lee, S. (1990). *Teacher research: From promise to power.* Katonah, NY: R. C. Owen.

Perl, S. (1979). Composing processes of unskilled college writers. *Research in the Teaching of English, 13,* 317–336.

Petraglia, J. (2000). Interrupting the conversation: The constructionist dialog in composition. In L. Worsham, S. Dobrin, & G. Olson (Eds.), *The Kinneavy papers: Theory and the study of discourse* (pp. 95–117). Albany: State University of New York Press and Association of Teachers of Advanced Composition.

Philips, S. (1972). Acquisition of roles for appropriate speech usage. In R. Abrahams & R. Troike (Eds.), *Language and cultural diversity in American education* (pp. 167–183). Englewood Cliffs, NJ: Prentice-Hall.

Piestrup, A. (1973). Black dialect interference and accommodation of instruction in the first grade. Monographs of the *Language Behavior Research Laboratory, No. 4*. Berkeley: University of California.

Pinker, S. (1997). *How the mind works*. New York: W. W. Norton.

Rabinow, P., & Sullivan, W. (Eds.). (1979). *Interpretive social science: A reader*. Berkeley, CA: University of California Press.

Ritchie, J. (1989). Beginning writers: Diverse voices and individual identity. *College Composition and Communication, 40*(2), 152–174.

Ritchie, J., & Wilson, D. (2000). *Teacher narrative as critical inquiry: Rewriting the script*. New York: Teachers College Press.

Rist, R. (1973). *The urban school: Factory for failure*. Cambridge, MA: MIT Press.

Rose, M. (1989). *Lives on the boundary*. New York: Macmillan Free Press.

Rose, M., & Hull, G. (1990). Toward a social cognitive understanding of problematic writing. In A. Lunsford, H. Moglen, & J. Slevin (Eds.), *The right to literacy*. New York: MLA.

Rosen, H. (1978). Toward a language policy across the curriculum. In D. Barnes, J. Britton, & H. Rosen (Eds.), *Language, the learner, and the school* (Rev. ed., p. 141). London: Penguin.

Rosenblatt, L. (1983). *Literature as exploration* (4th ed.). New York: Modern Language Association. (Original work published in 1938)

Rozin, P. S., & Gleitman, L. (1977). The structure and acquisition of reading II: The reading process and the acquisition of the alphabetic principle. In S. Reber & D. Scarborough (Eds.), *Toward a psychology of reading* (pp. 55–107). New Jersey: Lawrence Erlbaum.

Ruddell, R. (1974). A communication framework for the reading language teacher. In *Reading language instruction: Innovative practices* (pp. 28–48). Englewood Cliffs, NJ: Prentice Hall.

Schegloff, E. (1982). Discourse as an interactional achievement: Some uses of "uh huh" and other things that come between sentences. In D. Tannen (Ed.), *Analyzing discourse: Text and talk* (pp. 71–93). Georgetown University Round Table on Languages and Linguistics. Washington, DC: Georgetown University Press.

Scholes, R. (1985). *Textual power: Literary theory and the teaching of English*. New Haven, CT: Yale University Press.

Scollon, R., & Scollon, S. (1981). *Narrative, literacy, and face in interethnic communication*. Norwood, NJ: Ablex.

Scribner, S., & Cole, M. (1981). *The psychology of literacy*. Cambridge, MA: Harvard University Press.

Searle, J. (1975). Indirect speech acts. In E. Cole & J. Morgan (Eds.), *Syntax and semantics* (pp. 59–82). New York: Academic Press.

Shaughnessy, M. H. (1977). *Errors and expectations: A guide for the teacher of basic writing*. New York: Oxford University Press.

Simons, H. (1979). Black dialect, reading interference, and social interaction. In

L. Resnick & P. Weaver (Eds.), *Theory and practice of early reading,* vol. 3, (pp. 111–129). Hillsdale, NJ: Lawrence Erlbaum.

Simons, H. D., & Murphy, S. (1986). Spoken language strategies and reading acquisition. In J. Cook-Gumperz (Ed.), *The social construction of literacy* (pp. 186–204). Cambridge: Cambridge University Press.

Singer, H., & Ruddell, R. (Eds.). (1976). *Theoretical models and processes of reading* (2nd ed.). Newark, DE: International Reading Association.

Skinner, B. F. (1967). Thinking. In L. Jakobovitz & M. Miron (Eds.), *Readings in the psychology of language* (pp. 128–147). Englewood Cliffs, NJ: Prentice-Hall.

Smitherman, G. (1977). *Talkin' and testifyin': The language of Black America.* Boston: Houghton Mifflin.

Smitherman, G., & Villanueva, V. (Eds.). (2003). *Language diversity in the classroom: From intention to practice. Studies in writing and rhetoric.* Carbondale: Southern Illinois University Press.

Sohn, K. (2006) *Whistlin' and crowin' women of Appalachia: Literacy practices since college.* Carbondale: Southern Illinois University Press.

Stein, A. (1971). Strategies for failure. *Harvard Educational Review, 41,* 158–204.

Stein, G. (1935). Pictures. In *Lectures in America* (pp. 59–90). New York: Random House.

Stewart, W. (1972). On the use of Negro dialect in the teaching of reading. In R. Abrahams & R. Troike (Eds.), *Language and cultural diversity in American education* (pp. 262–274). Englewood Cliffs, NJ: Prentice-Hall.

Stock, P. (2001). Toward a theory of genre in teacher research: Contributions from a reflective practitioner. *English Education, (33)*2, 100–114.

Street, B. V. (1984). Introduction. In *Literacy in theory and practice.* Cambridge: Cambridge University Press.

Students' Right to Their Own Language. (1974, Fall). *College Composition and Communication, 25.*

Tannen, D. (1985). Relative focus on involvement in oral and written discourse. In D. Olson, N. Torrance, & A. Hildyard (Eds.), *Literacy, language, and learning: The nature and consequences of reading and writing.* Cambridge: Cambridge University Press.

Tateishi, C. (Ed.). (2001–2002). *Bay Area Writing project teacher research program: Working papers of teacher researchers.* Berkeley: University of California.

Tripp, D. (1993). *Critical incidents in teaching: Developing personal judgements.* London: Routledge.

Tuman, M. (1987). *Preface to literacy: An inquiry into pedagogy, practice, and progr/* Tuscaloosa: University of Alabama.

Vygotsky, L. S. (1962). *Thought and language* (E. Hanfmann & G. Vakar, F Trans.). Cambridge, MA: MIT.

Vygotsky, L. S. (1978). *Mind in society: The development of higher psycholo*s.). *cesses* (M. Cole, V. John-Steiner, S. Scribner, & E. Souberman, Eds. a*r* Cambridge, MA: Harvard University Press.

Wertsch, J. (2000). Vygotsky's two minds on the nature of meaning. In C. L*through* rinsky (Eds.), *Vygotskian perspectives on literacy research: Constructing collaborative inquiry* (pp. 19–30). Cambridge: Cambridge Universit* behavior.*

Whiting, B., & Whiting, J. (1973). Methods for observing and re*thropology* In R. Naroll & R. Cohen (Eds.), *A handbook of method in c*' (pp. 282–315). New York: Columbia University Press.

Williams, A. (1972). Dynamics of a Black audience. In T. Kochman (Ed.), *Rappin' and stylin' out: Communication in urban Black America* (pp. 32–64). Urbana: University of Chicago Press.

Williams, F. (1970). Language attitude and social change. In *Language and poverty: Perspectives on a theme* (pp. 380–396). Chicago: Markham Press.

Wilson, M. (1988). *The role of student–teacher interaction in the production of written compositions.* Unpublished doctoral dissertation, University of California, Berkeley.

Wolcott, H. (1990). *Writing up qualitative research.* Newbury Park, CA: Sage.

Yngve, V. (1970). On getting a word in edgewise. In *Papers from the Sixth Regional Meeting of the Chicago Linguistic Society* (pp. 567–577). Chicago: Chicago Linguistic Society.

Zebroski, J. (1994). *Thinking through theory: Vygotskian perspectives on the teaching of writing.* Portsmouth, NH: Boynton/Cook, Heinemann.

Index

About the Author

Smokey Wilson has been working with academically inexperienced adult learners throughout her career as instructor and director of the Tutorial Center at Laney College, an inner-city community college in Oakland California; as co-founder (with Bruce Jacobs and Marlene Griffith) and co-coordinator (with Margot Dashiell) of the basic skills learning community known as Project Bridge; and as founder and coordinator of an ASL/English bilingual/bicultural program called Deaf College Access Network (DeafCAN).

She also has been an educational consultant and curriculum developer for Academic Systems Software Corporation, the Walter and Elise Hass Foundation, and the Bay Area Writing Project.

With both a Bachelor's and Master's degree in English literature from the University of Arizona, Wilson later earned a second M.A. and a Ph.D. in Language and Literacy at the University of California (Berkeley). Her publications include an early freshman composition text entitled *Struggles with Bears: Experience in Writing*, and numerous articles that deal with the questions and answers discussed in this volume.

She lives in Oakland, California, and has three children: John, James, and Martena. Pets and plants are her pleasures; literacy is her passion.